OUR VANISHING PRIVACY

AND WHAT YOU CAN DO TO PROTECT YOURS

Robert Ellis Smith
Publisher, *Privacy Journal*

Loompanics Unlimited
Port Townsend, WA 98368

This book is sold for information purposes only. Neither the author nor the publisher will be held accountable for the use or misuse of the information contained in this book.

Our Vanishing Privacy
© 1993 by Robert Ellis Smith

Published by:
Loompanics Unlimited
PO Box 1197
Port Townsend, WA 98368

Loompanics Unlimited is a division of Loompanics Enterprises, Inc.

Cover design by George Lallas.

ISBN 1-55950-100-6
Library Of Congress Catalog Card Number 93-77301

CONTENTS

Chapter One
Before It's Too Late

Why is it that Americans care about personal privacy? *Or do they?*

Every public-opinion survey shows that privacy ranks high among Americans' concerns. But it never ranks at the very top. For good reason. There are other competing values that Americans hold dear — education for their children, good health care, strong law enforcement, efficient government, pursuing a career.

The fact is that Americans are ambivalent about privacy and information gathering. Europeans have shown a greater assertiveness in regulating personal data banks.

By day, most of us earn our livings collecting or disseminating information of one sort or another. By night, as consumers and citizens, we complain about intrusions into our privacy.

Throughout our history, we Americans have been intensely curious. We even wrote into our Constitution a requirement that we take a census every decade. Visitors who come here from elsewhere usually comment on Americans' curiosity about the personal lives of strangers — and our great willingness to share facts about ourselves with others.

This has created an insatiable appetite for information. We are never more than 15 minutes away from news reports, either by air or in print. We find ourselves absorbed in the personal lives of politicians, athletes, and celebrities. We feel insecure at work if we don't have every bit of information at our fingertips.

In spite of our ire about increased intrusiveness in our lives, we seem to halt at the point of limiting personal information gathering, either by legislation or consumer choices.

Most of our privacy concerns focus on commercial intrusions into our lives — mailing lists, unwanted telephone calls, credit reports, demands by insurance companies and lenders. In our minds there seems to be a link between protecting privacy and avoiding the over-commercialism of life in America.

We are constantly assaulted by advertising everywhere we go, demands to consume and to consume some more. We expect that our homes will be safe havens from the assaults. But that is no longer the case. Automated dialing devices and recorded messages allow telemarketers to intrude upon our living space at will. Our home entertainment is saturated with demands to spend money. Our daily mail is polluted with advertising.

People call it privacy, but what they really seem to be seeking is freedom from manipulation in the marketplace.

The current crisis has been created because of advances in technology. This is true of an earlier crisis in personal privacy 100 years ago.

For the first 100 years of our nation's history, our ambiguity about privacy and information was left in the background. There was certainly plenty of land for everyone ("Go West, young man!"). Gossip went no further than the next village. If we made a mistake, our neighbors would likely forgive us; they knew our roots.

At the end of the previous century, technological developments changed that. Crowded cities, the telephone and telegraph, photography, high-speed newspaper printing, tabloid journalism — all created a realization that individuals needed a physical or psychological space for escape, for one to be oneself.

Two lawyers from Boston gave voice to this concern in 1890. "Recent inventions and business methods call attention to the next step which must be taken for the protection of the person," wrote Louis D. Brandeis and Samuel D. Warren in advocating legal protection of "the right to be let alone."

"Gossip is no longer the resource of the idle and of the vicious, but has become a trade, which is pursued with industry as well as effrontery," Warren and Brandeis wrote in 1890, in a passage that could apply to the credit reporting and demographic marketing of the 1990s.

Can the concept of "privacy" encompass our quest for solitude, our frustration with credit reports and direct mail, the trivialization of gossip journalism, *and* the over-commercialization of the 1990s? What is the connecting link among them?

A century ago, Warren and Brandeis identified it. "It both belittles and perverts. It belittles by inverting the relative importance of things, thus dwarfing the thoughts and aspirations of a people."

- Devoting valuable computer innovation merely to segment Americans and sell them products they do not need perverts our economy.
- Obsessing about celebrities' intimacies belittles our culture. It demeans the achievements of public figures. It distracts us from the realities in our own lives.
- Filling our news media with trivial details and fabrications about other peoples' lives diverts us from meeting the needs of the nation.
- Relying on massive computer data bases deceives us into thinking that they are actually solving our problems or deterring fraud.
- Insisting that the whole population be enumerated and forced to carry plastic ID documents destroys the freedom and the spontaneity of life. It perverts the very purpose of America.

And so, privacy is vital to our national life. Otherwise our culture is debased, belittled, and perverted.

It is equally crucial to the lives of each one of us. Without privacy, there is no safe haven to know oneself. There is no space for experimentation, risk-taking, and making mistakes. There is no room for growth. Without privacy there is no introspection; there is only group activity. Without privacy, everyone resembles everyone else. A number will do, not a name or a personality. Without privacy, individuality perishes. Without individuality, there can be no group culture, or at least no group culture with any merit.

As we approach the Twenty-First Century we must reinvigorate the idea of personal privacy so that we maintain a proper balance between privacy and the values that compete with it. The 20 principles for information privacy and the principles for press coverage in this book are intended to help us reach that balance.

As citizens and as consumers, we must force government agencies and businesses to ask:

"Do we need to ask for the information in the first place?"

"Can we safeguard the information?"

"Will we use the information only for its original purpose?"

"Will asking for more personal information actually help solve the problem we perceive?"

"Can we survive if choice and autonomy are preserved in American life?"

"Can we protect individual privacy, before it's too late?"

Chapter Two
Are Your Papers In Order?

Writing 60 years ago, the French poet and critic Paul Valery noted: "Among living intellects, some spend themselves in serving the machine, others in building it, others in inventing or planning a more powerful type; a final category of intellects spend themselves in trying to escape its domination. These rebellious minds feel with a shudder that the once complete and autonomous whole that was the soul of ancient man is now becoming some inferior kind... that wishes only to collaborate, to join the crowd, to find security in being dependent..."

Valery went on to observe: "The most redoubtable machines, perhaps, are not those that revolve or run, to transport or transform matter or energy. There are other kinds, not built of copper or steel but of narrowly specialized individuals: I refer to organizations, those administrative machines constructed in imitation of the *impersonal aspects of the mind.*"[1]

We should remember that the laureates of the cybernetic nightmare — Kafka, Orwell, Huxley — were in fact rebelling against impersonal bureaucracies more than computerization. The anti-utopias in George Orwell's *1984,* Yevgeny Zamyatin's *We,* and Aldous Huxley's *Brave New World,* are *bureaucratic* tyrannies, not necessarily *computerized* tyrannies.

The "need" for a national identity document or for increased uses of Social Security numbers in America comes from these bureaucracies, which now dominate our society. When we weigh the convenience of bureaucracies against the inherent rights of Americans to autonomy and independence, the choice should be clear.

A mandatory national identity document, as proposed in Congress from time to time, would remove most of the flexibility from American life. Our founding fathers — Jefferson, Adams, Madison — spoke of the need for solitude and reflection. You cannot practice these when you are accountable to your government whenever you stray from your house. From William Penn to Henry David Thoreau to Walt Whitman to Horace Greeley, our essayists have cried out for more elbow room.

America stands today as one of the very few places where citizens have the freedom to travel without in-

---

[1]*The Collected Works of Paul Valery* (Princeton University Press, 1962), quoted in *Fairy Tales for Computers,* edited by Leslie George Katz (The Eakins Press, Boston, 1978).

ternal controls *and* vast open spaces in which to exercise that freedom.

The right to travel in America "may be as close to the heart of the individual as the choice of what he eats, or wears, or reads," said our Supreme Court in 1958. Associate Justice Sandra Day O'Connor wrote in 1983, "Our Constitution is designed to maximize individual freedom within a framework of ordered liberty."

But we all take that for granted. What has happened to the spontaneity of American life? The informality? The association with the natural environment? The freedom? In the second half of this century, have we traded it for convenience and accountability?

Throughout our history our most creative impulses have emerged out of risk-taking, out of a freedom to make mistakes, even out of chaos. They have not been generated when we have been observed, recorded, and enumerated.

Some bureaucrats insist that the country would run more smoothly if we all were compelled to carry a unique, counterfeit-proof plastic identity card. They seem to forget that a large number of Americans — or their parents — came to the United States to escape oppressive requirements that they always carry their "papers" with them.

In the past 60 years, the instincts of the American people have been right about the matter of mandatory enumeration. When the Social Security system was established, there were intense concerns about the possibility that the Social Security number could become a de facto national identifier. (Legislators promised this would never happen. They promised also that Social Security numbers would be used only for Social Security purposes.) Americans at that time were aware of the abuses of Nazi Germany.

In spite of constant concerns about crime and fraud and illicit dealings, the American people are still wary of a national identity document. In an opinion survey by Louis Harris in 1990, 56 percent of those questioned opposed the idea of even a national work identification card to distinguish between illegal aliens and citizens or resident aliens. Polls in Australia show that opposition will increase sharply as a proposal for a national identity card becomes known.

Older Americans, who remember the Nazi experience, are probably more wary of enumeration than younger people, who have grown up in the Seventies and Eighties with plastic cards and multi-digit numbers. We should remember that the last great uprising in this country (in the Sixties) began not with the cry, "Stop the War," but a few years earlier with the chant in Berkeley, California: "I am a Student. Do Not Fold Bend or Mutilate."

Elected politicians sense this reluctance in the American character, and so most of them disguise their endorsement of the idea of a national identity document. Bureaucrats sense this opposition as well. Being bureaucrats, they press not for a national ID number immediately but for authority to enumerate only their own constituency, to serve their narrow needs — without regard to the cumulative impact of these gradual intrusions on the citizenry as a whole.

And so the nightmare of a national ID number is upon us, because of a series of small bureaucratic baby steps, not as the result of a deliberate national decision.

"A national ID card," the bureaucrats say, "would be used only for employers to establish citizenship. It would not be used to cash checks. Police could not require you to produce it on the street. We'll make sure by legislation." But is it realistic to expect that such a policy would last long?

Even without a mandatory national ID number, we already have enough horror stories to give us a glimpse of what will happen to millions of Americans. The following cases actually happened:

An innocent black man is stopped and arrested 15 times in two years while walking in a white neighborhood, merely because he does not produce "bona fide identification."

A Washington woman is put off an Amtrak train in Philadelphia because she is unable to produce a driver's license, even though she paid for her ticket in cash.

A man jogging in Washington is detained by police because he is not carrying identification.

The affluent community of Palm Beach, Florida, tries to require by ordinance that non-residents employed in the town carry identity cards and produce them upon demand.

A parish in Louisiana tries to require "itinerant laborers" to register and carry ID cards.

A Native American parent is required to obtain a Social Security number for his four-year-old daughter even though this violates his sincerely held religious beliefs.

A Chicago woman, after making an illegal left turn, is locked up in the city jail and strip-searched because she could not locate her driver's license.

The water company in Hackensack, New Jersey, tries to require each of its customers to identify, by Social Security numbers and relationships, every single person living in the household.

A Nebraska woman is compelled to spend thousands of dollars in legal fees to protect her right to have a driver's license without foregoing her sincerely held religious belief against being photographed.

The school system in Tulsa requires a pupil of any age to provide a Social Security number before attending classes.

Police officers in California demand Social Security numbers of persons arrested for traffic offenses.

In California and elsewhere, a person must be fingerprinted before receiving a driver's license.

The largest bank in the U.S., Citibank, answers its toll-free customer account line not with "Hello," but, "What is your Social Security number?"

Is this our vision of America? Or is it closer to the wartime Netherlands of Anne Frank?

A national ID card won't work. We know from experience that there is no such thing as a tamper-proof identity document.

As shopkeepers, police officers, and bureaucrats are led to believe that the new document is counterfeit-proof, they will place increasing reliance on the validity of the ID card. This will simply raise the ante on the street for more sophisticated phony IDs.

Our current willy-nilly system of non-identification may seem unreliable to many; but that may be its strength. At least most of us know better than to place great faith in the validity of current IDs. Some us are not lulled into a false sense of security. We know, or should know, that the best assurance of identity is personal recognition — or its close substitutes.

Reliance on numbers deceives us into thinking we have accurately established identity. We need only look to those institutions in American life that are most intensively enumerated now — prisons, the military, corporate America, colleges and universities. In each of these segments, identifying — and enumerating — the population is not difficult. Yet these are places where crime and fraud occur at a rate higher than — or at least as high as — in the population as a whole.

James Q. Wilson, the law-enforcement expert at UCLA, makes the point that we *know* who the criminals are in each community. They keep committing the same crimes over and over again. Police departments know who they are. It's not as if the police need to place a number on each criminal in order to know who they are. (Ex-cons, after all, are tagged with a number and are pretty well known to law enforcement, and yet they commit most of the crimes.) Nor is it common that criminals use correct Social Security numbers or leave their true IDs at the scene of the crime.

Organizations insist on Social Security numbers mainly out of laziness. It's a number that most people can remember. Demanding the number is a way of persuading people that they can be tracked down after any wrongdoing — a bounced check, an inflated resume, a failure to report income to tax authorities.

Yet, in the 1990s, large organizations have the capability to store and retrieve massive amounts of personal data without resorting to Social Security numbers or any other numbers. MIB Inc. (the Medical Information Bureau), which stores medical codes on more than 11 million insured Americans, is an example. IBM Corp. long ago abandoned SSNs as employee numbers for its thousands of personnel.

It is not news that the Social Security number has become a virtual mandatory national identity number

— even if it is a seriously flawed one. What is news is that there may now be alternative routes toward the much-feared national ID:

Several companies — like United Parcel Service and Matsushita — are using a bar code, like the black and white Uniform Product Code on groceries, that contains letters as well as numbers. UPS wants to use its own variation of the bar code to include names, addresses, and routing information. Using similar technology, some states would like to add a bar code to drivers' licenses. A bar code could be issued to each man, woman, and child in the U.S., encoding name, address, and even personal information.

Bellcore, the research arm of AT&T, is developing a concept called PNC, Personal Number Calling. This would permit the same phone number to be used for home phone, vacation home, office, modem, auto phone, pager, and fax machine. One PNC could be issued for the duration of your life, a means to summon you anywhere.

The U.S. Postal Service has already expanded the zip code to nine digits, with each number targeting a group of 200 people or fewer. Now the Postal Service is expanding the zip code further, so that a distinct number could be assigned to virtually every address in the U.S. As part of the plan, the USPS is creating a list of every known address in the U.S.

Urged on by the Federal Bureau of Investigation, states are building data banks of individual genetic codes (DNA "fingerprints"), which are said to be unique for each individual. The current thinking is to require these codes only of those convicted of violent crimes. But University of Colorado sociologist Gary T. Marx asks, "Through a process of 'surveillance creep,' will this spread to those convicted of non-violent crimes? And will mandatory genetic 'fingerprinting' eventually be required of the population at large?"

While we have been worried about the Social Security number as a form of national ID, we have not realized that a national identifier may come from other sources.

It is ironic that in the same decade that we Americans rejoice in the liberation of peoples in Eastern Europe we are seriously considering adopting a means of social control that Eastern Europeans rejected soundly.

As we encourage the dismantling of apartheid in South Africa, we continue the drift in our own country to a "domestic passport" similar to that required in South Africa.

After going to war with a regime in the Middle East that categorizes and oppresses its people, can we seriously be considering a plan that could have no other purpose in our own country?

The late J. Braxton Craven Jr., of the U.S. Fourth Circuit Court of Appeals, spoke of "personhood," not "privacy," when categorizing the unenumerated Constitutional rights that make Americans special. In reference to the right of personhood, Judge Craven wrote:

"To the average person, who may not wish to make a speech or print a newspaper, it may be the greatest freedom of all. The right to be let alone is the only non-political protection for that vast array of human activities which, considered separately, may seem trivial, but together make up what most individuals think of as freedom. I am thinking of little things, mostly taken for granted, such as the right to attend a football game, to refrain from attending a political rally, to wear a hat, or to ride a bicycle to work through city traffic."[2]

Now, will we require a plastic card to engage, or not engage, in these simple pursuits of "personhood?" Will we do this in the name of keeping undocumented aliens from our menial jobs or in the name of preventing a few from double-dipping into our inadequate public-assistance payments?

If we do, we will lose the soul of America.

---

[2] J. Braxton Craven, "Personhood: The Right to be Let Alone," 1976 *Duke Law Journal* 699.

Chapter Three
Your Social Security Number: Guard It With Your Life

In the summer of 1990 a California woman sat down with an appeals officer in the Internal Revenue Service. "Just because I didn't put Social Security numbers for my children on my tax return," said Suzanne Watson, "doesn't mean that they don't exist."

An IRS auditor had disallowed the woman's exemptions for her three dependents and deductions for some of her child-care expenses. The auditor was relying on a 1988 law that requires parents to list Social Security numbers on any children they claim as dependents. Congress passed the law because the IRS suspects that many divorced parents are claiming the same child as a dependent (even though obviously only one of them is providing more than half of the support, as required by law).

Suzanne Watson (not her real name) won over the IRS appeals officer, who has the authority to overrule an auditor. The appeals officer permitted the deductions rather than forcing the woman to go to Tax Court to prove her point.

The woman based her objection on religious beliefs. Like many fundamentalist Christians, she relies on a Biblical passage warning that whoever worships a Satanic beast that issues a mark or number to all persons will incur the wrath of God.

Other people base their objection to being enumerated by Social Security numbers on their right to privacy. They simply resent being labeled with a government number. This objection is usually not as successful as the religious argument. And the religious argument is not always successful. The IRS decision in California affects only that one taxpayer, and the U.S. Supreme Court ruled in 1986 that a Native American's religious objection, though "sincerely held," did not prevent the state welfare authorities from demanding a Social Security number on his daughter.

Most people's objections are far more pragmatic: They sense that a person's Social Security number is the key to finding out information about that person from the many databases in government agencies and private businesses. They sense too that the number is the means for linking these databases so that an organization can pool lots of personal information about someone without the individual ever knowing about it.

Think of the organizations that have your Social Security number: the Internal Revenue Service, your employer, your health insurance company, the military, state motor vehicle departments, banks, government agencies, hospitals and doctors, schools, and colleges. And then there are the extraneous demands, which border on the ridiculous: to get a check-cashing card in a supermarket, to get a fishing license, to register to vote, to donate blood, to arrange a funeral, to sign up for cable TV, and even to enter a radio station's contest.

Some of the uses of Social Security numbers are downright dangerous — like labeling your personal goods in your home as part of a police burglary-prevention program. Some are stupid — like using it as a military ID number. Once, a prisoner in Fort Leavenworth, Kansas, developed a flourishing business in filing false income tax returns for refunds; he used other persons' Social Security numbers that he took off discarded military uniforms he was assigned to sort as part of his prison work.

When the Social Security system was established, there were concerns about all of this. After President Roosevelt permitted use of the SSN as a taxpayer number, the trend toward making it a de facto national identity number hastened. Employers, of course, needed the number, as did anyone else with whom you had a taxable transaction.

Until the 1960s, Social Security cards bore the legend NOT FOR IDENTIFICATION, and this led many Americans to believe that it was illegal to use the SSN for non-Social Security purposes. But that has never been true.

In 1973, a special task force in the U.S. Department of Health, Education, and Welfare warned against abuses of the numerical identifier. Its recommendations led to a provision in the Privacy Act of 1974 that prohibits a federal, state, or local government agency from collecting a Social Security number from anyone unless the agency can point to a law or regulation *already on the books in 1974* permitting use of the number. A couple of years later, Congress reacted to complaints from state bureaucrats and exempted state motor-vehicle departments, welfare departments, and tax departments from that provision of the federal Privacy Act.

There never have been any laws limiting private businesses from collecting or using Social Security numbers. In fact, more and more laws and regulations since 1974 *permit* or *require* some of them to do so.

So what are our protections now? Government agencies may deny a person a benefit for failure to produce an SSN only if they can show a law or regulation permitting them to gather this information. In any case, a government agency has to tell you why it is requesting your number and what it will do with it.

School systems ask for Social Security numbers. But public school systems and state universities are part of state government, and they are subject to the prohibition in the Privacy Act of 1974 on Social Security numbers. Most state agencies, especially schools and universities, ignore the requirements of the Privacy Act or have devised interesting loopholes.

Any entity — government or non-government — that has a transaction with you that must be reported to tax authorities seems to have a legitimate need for your number. This includes employers, banks, lenders, stockbrokers, and private and public insurers (but only when they are paying out money to you). In fact, financial institutions get fined if they don't list your Social Security number on government paperwork.

Because the banking system relies heavily on Social Security numbers to keep track of depositors and, to a lesser extent, the insurance industry uses them to keep track of policyholders, credit bureaus like to collect Social Security numbers.

Credit bureaus are really the central switchboard in the whole personal information network. They gather information on credit applications from stores, credit-card companies, and other retailers and each month are notified how you are paying your bills. In turn, they provide other businesses with payment histories on applicants for credit or employment.

Life is easier for credit bureaus if they have Social Security numbers on all consumers, especially because one of their greatest problems is keeping straight consumers with similar names. That is why you are asked for a Social Security number whenever you apply for credit. But there is no requirement that you give it. In these cases, the last four digits of a SSN should be adequate to prevent duplication, or the credit bureaus could create an alternative number themselves.

There are real dangers to disclosing your Social Security number to just anyone. It should be guarded as carefully as your telephone credit-card number, your travel and entertainment card number, or the personal ID number for your automatic teller card.

With your Social Security number, other people can more easily — with or without authority — access these data banks that keep information on you. For instance, "computer hackers" — many of them not yet out of high school — have purchased Social Security numbers in an underground electronic network and then cracked the data system of TRW credit bureau. They then "steal" the clean credit of someone else or merely steal the credit-card numbers of people listed in TRW files and order products on those persons' credit-card accounts.

Private investigators often get information on people they are investigating by discovering their Social Security numbers and impersonating them over the telephone. A legendary private eye named Ike Eisenhauer once told an investigating committee in Canada how with a person's Social Insurance Number, as it is called in Canada, he "feigned confusion" over the telephone while posing as the person he was investigating. Before long he had coaxed from the governmental insurance program the home and office addresses and phone number of the person he was trying to locate.

Another investigator who levies liens against bank accounts in California says that with a person's bank account number and Social Security number, he can easily learn that person's account balances over the telephone. "I can monitor your account daily," he says. "I can determine the best time to attach that account for maximum recovery."

In 1991, many consumer-protection offices around the country became aware of a scam in which telephone marketers ask consumers for their checking-account numbers so that the telemarketers can process a monthly automatic withdrawal from those accounts. An alternative version of this scam is to ask for a Social Security number (which most consumers are more willing to provide) and then to use the SSN to persuade a bank officer to provide a checking-account number.

"It is imperative that consumers exercise extreme caution when anyone requests personal information from them such as their checking account number, Social Security number, address, date of birth or any other information relative to credit," warned former Rhode Island Attorney General James E. O'Neil in 1991.

So what is a consumer to do when asked for a Social Security number?

♦ Don't put your number on an employment application; wait until you are hired.

- Do provide a Social Security number to an agency that will be paying you a salary or interest or dividends, charging you interest, or maintaining a checking or savings account for you.
- Do remember that state motor vehicle departments, tax departments, and welfare departments are authorized to demand an SSN. Otherwise, do not provide a Social Security number to any government agency unless it provides you with its authority to do so and its uses for the number.
- Try not to provide your number to the motor vehicles office unless it insists on it; in many states the motor vehicles department will waive its original demand for a SSN. Even if you must provide it, try to avoid having your SSN used as your driver's license number and printed on your license.
- Use caution when you are asked for your Social Security number by a retail store, a utility company, a private college, an insurance company, a credit-card company, or other private business. No law says you have to give it; no law says the company has to do business with you. Try providing only the last four digits. Or provide the number with a statement asking that it not be disclosed further. Ask that the number not appear on mailing labels.
- Don't provide your SSN when you cash a check or pay by credit card. Make clear why you are objecting.
- Don't provide your Social Security number over the telephone.
- Avoid enumerating your child at an early age. Most requests for SSNs by public school systems are not enforceable.
- Remember that federal law requires a Social Security number on your tax return for any child two years or older claimed as a dependent. Federal law

requires that a child receiving Aid to Families with Dependent Children (AFDC) have a Social Security number. And some states require *parents'* Social Security numbers on applications for birth certificates (but not on the actual certificate itself). If you feel strongly about not enumerating your children, you can waive your claim to a tax deduction. Or, like Suzanne Watson in California, you can battle the IRS and perhaps win.

Chapter Four
Even The Post Office

In the computer age, privacy has been defined as the right to control when and how information about oneself will be collected, used, and disclosed.[1]

In earlier times, each of us may have thought that our names and addresses hardly needed to be kept secret; this, after all, is basic information about ourselves that our fellow citizens are entitled to know. For the past two decades, the Postal Service has operated under that assumption.

But that trusting attitude is no longer possible.

Even though your address may have been regarded as public in the past, it has not until now been readily

---

[1] Alan F. Westin, *Privacy and Freedom* (Atheneum, 1967).

available from an instant, centralized source. As the U.S. Supreme Court said in 1990, "There is a vast difference [in privacy considerations] between the public records that might be found in a diligent search of courthouse files, county archives and local police stations throughout the country and a computerized summary located in a single clearinghouse of information."[2]

In addition, threats to our economic and personal security have become increasingly menacing in the 1990s — serial killing, kidnapping, child-snatching, acquaintance rape, sexual harassment, door-to-door swindles, adoption searches, and custody battles. The cautious person in the 1990s reveals one's residential address selectively. In other words, the wise person wants to *control when and how address information about oneself will be collected, used, and disclosed.*

Some examples of why that is important:

The man who stalked and then murdered TV actress Rebecca Schaeffer in her front yard in 1989 learned her home address through a simple check of motor vehicle lists in California. California now permits a person to provide an alternative "public address," like a box number or an attorney or other intermediary. After an identical crime in Arizona earlier, the state tightened access to motor vehicle registration lists.

A New York doctor in 1992 discovered the modus operandi of a credit-card fraud that victimized him and thousands of other Americans:

---

[2] *Department of Justice v. Reporters Committee for Freedom of the Press*, 489 US 749 (1989), a case in which the Supreme Court illogically declared a higher privacy protection for a person's *arrest records* than bank records, medical records, or sexual activity.

"First, the criminals steal a list of names and Social Security numbers from a payroll or personnel office. They then rent an apartment (to serve as a mailing address) and install phones (to serve as home phones and, with call forwarding, to serve as 'work phones' with a different phone exchange). They next fill out a batch of credit applications for companies that grant credit by mail....The [credit grantors] then send the applications to a large commercial bank (e.g. Citicorp in New York or BankOne in Ohio)... The banks use computers with modems to communicate with the computers at TRW and Equifax [credit bureaus]....BOTH TRW AND EQUIFAX CHANGE THE ADDRESS IN AN INDIVID-UAL'S CREDIT HISTORY SOLELY ON THE BASIS OF AN APPLICATION FOR A CREDIT CARD OR CREDIT LINE AND NOT ON THE BASIS OF AN EVEN CURSORILY VERIFIED ADDRESS. Thus this credit check results in a fraudulent address being entered into an unsuspecting victim's file." Equifax says that it has changed its way of changing addresses.

The birth mother in an open adoption decided later that she wanted to keep the child, tracked down the address of the adopted parents, and began picketing across the street from the residence.

A drifter discovered that a Maine couple was seeking the identity of their child placed for adoption long ago. He learned their address, claimed to be their son, had them pay his travel and lodging expenses, and later moved in with the couple. Only later was he discovered to be a fraud.

Protecting one's name and address is no longer a symptom of paranoia.

New practices by the U.S. Postal Service have widened the possibilities that the now-sensitive facts of our names and whereabouts will fall into the wrong hands.

1. The Postal Service employs about 20 private companies as licensees to process changes in its National Change of Address system (NCOA). Every two weeks, the Postal Service gives these licensees computerized change-of-address lists (generated from the forms filled out by postal customers when they notify the post office).

The licensees are *companies engaged in the direct-mail business.* Thus, direct mailers get first crack at these valuable address changes. The commercial interest is simply too large for these licensees to resist using this information for their own ends. Although NCOA license terms seem to prohibit a contractor from using NCOA names and addresses for any purpose other than correction, they do not prohibit a licensee from using NCOA to update names and addresses it already possesses. Nor do they seem to prohibit a licensee from using the addresses to retrieve telephone numbers from readily available software (and thus using a list of *phone numbers, not addresses*).

Does any postal customer expect when he or she innocently fills out a change-of-address card at the local post office that he or she is providing an address update to the nation's major mailers? (Some people have discovered that local postal personnel erroneously insist to customers that change-of-address information never leaves the post office.)

It is unwise to use direct-mail firms for this governmental function, and it is doubly unwise to use

TRW Target Marketing Division as an NCOA licensee. TRW operates one of the three major credit bureaus in the nation, keeping computerized records on the names, addresses, places of employment, salary estimates, and credit and bank accounts on millions of Americans. These files are available to a multitude of persons and companies, some of them responsible, some of them not — banks, retail stores, employers, insurance companies, used-car dealers, landlords, "super bureaus" and small "information brokers" (which pass on the information to anybody, including private investigators), computer hackers cracking these systems from the shelter of their teenage bedrooms, and credit-card scam artists.

TRW extracts personal information from these credit reports and provides it to its Target Marketing Division for developing targeted mail and telephone marketing lists. The Federal Trade Commission has said this practice violates the Fair Credit Reporting Act. TRW's major competitor, Equifax (CBI), has discontinued the practice. Equifax, which operates a major nationwide credit bureau and a major marketing-list operation, is also an NCOA licensee.

Having access to NCOA address changes simply aids and abets TRW's abuses in this area. (TRW Target Marketing sells lists of "new movers" and blatantly advertises NCOA as the source for that product.)

2. The Postal Service's proposal in 1990 to update *and keep on file* a person's holiday mailing list showed insensitivity to privacy concerns. The Postal Service's intentions were perhaps honorable; it intended to correct each customer's greeting-card address list automatically before each holiday mailing. U.S. Representative Bob Wise of West Virginia said at the time, "The permanent maintenance of a customer

mailing list is a dangerous invasion of privacy. It is a threat both to those who send mail using this program and to those who receive it. For example, once the information becomes part of a system of records, it can be disclosed to law enforcement." This test program clearly violates the spirit of the provision of the Privacy Act that, "Each agency... shall... maintain no record describing how any individual exercises rights guaranteed by the First Amendment unless expressly authorized by statute or by the individual...." Do individuals realize that in asking for a simple cleaning of greeting-card lists, they are "authorizing" the U.S. Postal Service to keep track of whether they celebrate Christmas, Hanukkah, or Orthodox Easter?

3.   In spite of 200 years of tradition in the nation that law-abiding citizens may keep to themselves and may avoid "having their papers in order" and their whereabouts known, the Postal Service is developing a nationwide list of physical addresses. This file will not include names, it is said, and so at first glance it appears to be no threat to privacy. But, as the president of one the nation's largest direct marketers, R.R. Donnelley & Sons, told *The Wall Street Journal,* "It won't have your name on it unless I already have your name and address."

This scheme diminishes our privacy. The right to privacy includes a sense of autonomy, a right to develop a unique personality and living space, and a right to distinguish one's own persona from everyone else's. The Postal Service scheme will seek to eliminate duplicates, idiosyncrasies, and quaint misspellings or informality in street or place names. Those who find their identity in living in an alley, or on a dirt road, or on no road at all will have to fit their place names into some national mold. Already people in communities

across the nation are being told by fire departments, census takers, or postal employees that their place names or addresses just won't do, they will have to be changed to meet an acceptable, computerized standard.

An inevitable result of this master list will be more unsolicited telephone calls for Americans, after marketers match the Postal Service address list against software of phone numbers nationwide. CompuServe's "Phone*file" is one of the readily available products that will retrieve a phone number for a given address, without a name. Telematch is another.

4. The expanded, nine-digit zip code accelerates this trend. Because U.S. Census and other demographic data is refined at least to zip code, the expanded code serves only to enhance the precision with which marketers and manipulators can target the American people. National publications now alter their content and advertising to match the demographics of each zip code.

5. The Postal Service has felt compelled to go into business with one of the nation's other trustees of vital personal information, AT&T, in a joint venture called "Moving Solutions."

This is a voluntary offering to people planning to move. AT&T takes their new address and informs the local post office and magazine publishers, catalog companies, and other organizations that send the people mail regularly.

Moving Solutions' brochure boasts, "AT&T Moving Solutions and the U.S. Postal Service are working together to bring you more choices."

Why is this huge information company able to use the Postal Service's imprimatur and logo, which essentially belongs to the American people? Why is the Postal Service headquarters in Washington listed as the return address for Moving Solutions? Why does the USPS pay the postage for Moving Solutions advertising? Did anyone at the Postal Service understand the impropriety of a joint venture with AT&T, of all companies? To participate meaningfully in our society, all people must provide information about one's whereabouts and identity *to the phone company and the post office.* If these two entities view their use of this information as another sales opportunity, not a sacred trust, the American people have lost the assurance they need that these are responsible repositories of personal information.

Each of these incursions might be tolerable in themselves were they not part of a cumulative pattern by the Postal Service in the past two decades.

Some of these incursions might be tolerable if the Postal Service had scrutinized the privacy impact of them before proceeding.

All of these incursions might be tolerable were they necessary for our national security or for delivering services more efficiently to the American people or for knowing ourselves as a nation better.

But, in fact, these innovations by the Postal Service serve commercial clients, not the broad public interest. Both the Postal Service and the Bureau of the Census no longer serve the national interest; they have tailor-made their agendas (sometimes in concert with each other) to meet the needs of large commercial businesses. Most of both agencies' energies are now devoted to providing support for a few major businesses.

Beyond that, the Postal Service has no meaningful procedure for including privacy considerations in its policy making. That is why a Data Protection Board at the federal level, as proposed by Representative Wise,

is necessary. A board like this could articulate privacy considerations at the time national policies are being developed within federal agencies. It could insist that the privacy of the American people be part of any "cost-benefit analysis" in federal agencies.

is necessary. A board like this could articulate privacy considerations at the time national policies are being developed within federal agencies. It could insist that the privacy of the American people be part of any "cost-benefit analysis" in federal agencies.

Chapter Five
Caller ID:
My Privacy Or Yours?

Caller ID, which appears at first glance to enhance personal privacy, in fact diminishes telephone
customers' expectations of privacy. It could result in
serious adverse consequences, including personal danger, for telephone customers.

Caller ID displays the number of the telephone
where the incoming call was placed. Since 1990, it has
been offered mostly in the mid-Atlantic states, the
area served by Bell Atlantic telephone company.

The service, part of several new offerings by phone
companies made possible by new capabilities for
transmitting signals on telephone lines, is marketed as

a way of deterring unwanted calls — whether sales calls or anonymous obscene calls.

One of these other offerings is called Call Trace, which offers a safer, privacy-protective way of having the telephone company automatically and promptly trace the source of an harassing phone call.

In their infinite wisdom, telephone companies in some parts of the country have said that they will not offer Call Trace in states where they are denied permission to offer Caller ID. US West threatened that in Colorado, for instance. A computer enthusiast named John Gilbert points out, "Folks should get a good understanding here. US West is withholding Call Trace, something which *can* help fight malicious phone calls, and would be the same deterrent as Caller ID, because they want to deploy Caller ID under their own terms. While they probably have every right, understand that they have tied a useful service for us to a profitable one for them, despite public opposition to the one they like."

Caller ID, of course, permits operators of anonymous hotlines to know the phone number of a caller. It permits businesses to capture your phone number whenever you call for information, or a sample, or a product — or if you dial a wrong number. The long-distance equivalent of Caller ID — called Automatic Number Identification or ANI — has the same effect.

Does Caller ID violate legal principles of privacy? It does. A telephone company that discloses any sensitive information about a person or family (that can include telephone number and — indirectly — name, address, and demographic information) without consent may violate the privacy principles in a state constitution or in tort law as developed by a state legislature or court.

To the extent that this information is used commercially by other businesses, this could be a violation

of a recognized privacy principle against the commercial exploitation of a person's name, likeness, or persona. Mere "incidental" use of a name or other personal information may not violate these laws and court decisions, but a use "to attract the attention" of prospective buyers is clearly prohibited by this principle. "The appearance of an endorsement" is usually a necessary part of a claim for violation of these statutes, *but not always.* A case involving Hollywood actor Clint Eastwood established that principle.[1]

Displaying the incoming telephone number will permit unscrupulous businesses to engage in subtle and almost undetectable "redlining." If a business (a mortgage company, a taxi company, a lawn service, a florist) merely chose not to answer calls from a certain district, or to divert them to "hold" lines, or to charge them more, or to assign them to inexperienced staff, the victims would not even be aware of this.

Governmental investigations of redlining abuses would be virtually impossible. First, the authorities would need several complaints against the same business, but how would an individual victim know for sure that he or she had been treated unfairly? Next, law enforcement authorities would need to place a series of calls from several different neighborhoods (telephone exchanges), then prove that there was disparate treatment, based on the displayed incoming numbers.

Proving that a taxi company will not serve a certain neighborhood is relatively easy in today's telephone environment. If a dispatcher refuses a call once a person gives her or his address, the caller has a suspicion of discrimination. If a dispatcher, with Caller ID, chooses not to answer a call from a particular ad-

---

[1] *Eastwood v. Superior Court,* 149 Cal App 3rd 409, 198 Cal Rptr 342 (1983).

dress or to answer the phone by saying that no taxis are available, how is the victim put on notice of possible discrimination?

For businesses that use Caller ID or ANI, there is an opportunity to capture incoming telephone numbers for massive telemarketing uses, without the knowledge of the consumer. With Automatic Number Identification, a business can use the incoming number to retrieve stored name, address, and other customer information for in-house use. This practice seems not to raise privacy concerns, because the customer has an expectation that this is done and because there is no disclosure outside of the company.

But consider a company using Caller ID solely to collect telephone numbers of customers interested in a certain product or service. The company would not even need a telephone operator to answer calls. It would need only to advertise a product and a toll-free line. It would then capture the incoming phone numbers of persons who answer the ad. (Caller ID works even if the phone is not answered; it captures phone numbers as well as displays them.) The company would then sell to the highest bidder these lists of phone numbers along with customer preferences for certain products or services. This will generate countless telemarketing calls to consumers who were totally unaware that they had put themselves on the marketing lists!

Far-fetched? A company in Parsippany, New Jersey, called Touch Tone Access is selling precisely this service. "Our automatic caller identification option gives you additional direct follow-up opportunities," Touch Tone tells telemarketers in an advertisement in the trade press.

Touch Tone Access (which sells no products of its own) captures the phone numbers of callers to its toll-

free 800 lines, whether or not the phone is answered. Currently, it can also retrieve household addresses on 60 percent of the callers (through "Reverse Directory Appending"). It then builds a database of these names, addresses, and phone numbers, matched to demographic information about the caller (household income, make and model of automobile, ethnic group — data that is available from other sources) and matched to the particular services or products the caller inquired about. Touch Tone Access then provides this database to clients at 20 cents a name.

A customer who calls the 800 number may reconsider and say he or she does not wish to receive information on the product, but the person will still be added to the telemarketing list.

In addition, manufacturers are discovering that they can capture the names and phone numbers of callers to their 800 customer service numbers and use them "to sell more soap and soups."

"In fact, this is one of the main factors spurring the expansion of the '800' lines," according to *The New York Times.*

People in distress — escaping spousal or child abuse — will inadvertently provide information about their whereabouts because of Caller ID. Providing a blocking service to shelters and community-service organizations will not protect persons who call from a neighbor's house or any private residence. Runaway children will be reluctant to call home. In times of distress, people do not think to activate a blocking feature with each call, nor do they think to run to a public telephone, nor is it wise at these times for them to call from public telephones (where anonymous calling is possible).

Elderly people and children will be unlikely to activate a per-call blocking feature; yet they may be in a position to most need blocking protection.

Persons calling anonymous hotline services — for alcoholism, narcotics, other dependencies, abuse-prevention, AIDS, abortion or pregnancy, services for gay men and lesbians, employment placement, suicide-prevention, taxpayer assistance (including especially callers inquiring about amnesty offers) — will lose confidence in the total confidentiality and anonymity of these services, regardless of the sincerity of announcements by these public services that they do not have Caller ID capability or do not use it.

Professionals and others who make calls from their home phones to mentally ill, dangerous, or otherwise unstable persons will be vulnerable. This includes physicians, psychiatrists, psychologists, social workers, case workers, school teachers and principals, truancy officers, lawyers, private investigators, police investigators, tax collectors, bill collectors, and even other people whose names happen to come to public attention in an unpopular light. Officials at high levels of government and business will not be able to make telephone calls without revealing their direct office numbers or their home numbers, whether they are unlisted or not.

Aside from the privacy concerns, is Caller ID really useful?

It does not help the majority of persons who do not memorize more than one or two telephone numbers. The *name of the incoming caller* is helpful information and does not provide a numerical trail to the individual. The *number* of the caller is not helpful information to the average residential customer. It only provides an intrusive means of tracking the whereabouts of the

individual, as well as a means to match other data about the caller.

The reality is that after the novelty wears off, nearly all Caller ID subscribers will answer all telephone calls.

Caller ID promotes vigilantism. New Jersey Bell Co., in its advertisements promoting the offering, encourages the victims of obscene telephone calls *to call back the harassing caller with a threat, "I know your number!"*

Most law enforcement experts advise against engaging an obscene caller like this. Caller ID deludes customers into thinking that they are invulnerable to counterattack by the caller. It deludes them into thinking that by keeping a list of incoming calls from harassing callers (and their phone numbers) they can overcome the low priority police place on investigating obscene telephone calls.

New Jersey Bell claimed a 50-percent reduction in harassing calls in Hudson County, New Jersey, because of Caller ID. In fact, at the same time, New Jersey Bell introduced Call Trace, and so the deterrent effect can just as logically be attributed to Call Trace, not Caller ID.

Are there any benefits to this new Caller ID service?

The display of incoming telephone numbers for emergency 911 police dispatchers is a useful application; it permits police to trace the whereabouts of a caller who is incapacitated or unable to provide the information verbally. The chances of an incapacitated person calling the emergency line are high, and so the use of the technology is justified.

The display of incoming telephone numbers for retrieval of name, address, and account information is a benign, logical application for incoming telemarketers or telephone sales representatives. It saves time.

Such users, however, should not be able to market telephone numbers obtained through this technology, nor to market the identifying information that flows from number identification. There are two reasons for this: First, the customer is unaware of this capability and expects that the phone number will be kept confidential. Second, the telephone number that the customer provided for one purpose (billing and ordering) is now being used for a secondary purpose (outside marketing) without the consent of the individual.

Caller ID may deter obscene and other harassing callers who are "trapped" by it. The deterrent effect, however, will diminish, as unscrupulous individuals learn to circumvent it AND to turn it to *their advantage*. (In Baltimore, drug dealers learned not only how to defeat Caller ID but how to use it to their advantage by learning the numbers of their drug customers and returning the calls on a secure, untapped public telephone. This saves them the risk of answering a call on a possibly wiretapped line. In Portland, Maine, police report that drug dealers use Caller ID to recognize calls from undercover agents at police headquarters.)

On the other hand, there is a lot Caller ID won't do.

Caller ID cannot deter harassing calls from outside the local calling area, from cellular phones, from public phones, from outside the area code, from Centrex systems, from a business with a central switchboard, from strangers' residences and businesses, or calls where blocking has been activated. (The most notable case of sexually-abusive telephone calls in Washington, D.C. in the past few years involved a college president placing calls from his office; Caller ID cannot display these numbers.) That is a massive amount of excep-

tions to a service whose primary advantage is supposed to be the deterrence of nuisance calls.

Caller ID cannot deter harassing calls to persons whose curiosity will prompt them to answer calls from strangers. Isn't this the majority of people? A survey by GTE California Inc. found that 70 percent of customers are likely to answer a call even if a familiar number is not displayed.

Public utility commissions and consumer advocates around the country have pressured phone companies to offer a blocking capability when Caller ID is offered.

"Per-line blocking" blocks the display of your number on all calls made from your line. "Per call blocking" blocks the display of your number only when you remember to press *67 before the outgoing call.

The debates in the past five years have concerned: first, which form of blocking should be a required service by telephone companies and, second, whether blocking should be available free to anyone who wants it. The states of California, Maine, and North Dakota require free per-call blocking by law, and other states require it by regulatory action.

Permitting Caller ID with free per-call blocking provides the minimum consumer protection. This requires each telephone user, including young children, handicapped, and elderly persons, to make a decision upon dialing each call, "Will there be a need to protect my anonymity and my whereabouts on this call?" It is, of course, impossible to anticipate the answer to that question.

Once having made that decision, the caller is then burdened with pressing three additional numbers in order to activate the blocking feature. Persons used to dialing a telephone at work may often forget to dial *67 at home. Persons in distress — precisely those people who most need the protection of the blocking feature — will probably forget to do so altogether. These are people calling anonymous hotlines and people seeking shelter from domestic abuse.

Persons calling businesses will most likely not activate the blocking feature, because they will be unaware of the need to do so (both to avoid secondary telemarketing uses of their numbers and to foil redlining).

Each time, the caller must be alert, conscious of the need to protect anonymity. Is this realistic to expect in a residential setting?

Further, per-call blocking alone coupled with the phone companies' new Automatic Call Return could result in danger for recipients of harassing calls. Automatic Call Return allows a person to automatically dial back the last call received.

A harasser could dial numbers and just wait for his victims to call him back. If a person who is not home when the harasser called returned home and activated Automatic Call Return, the harasser with Caller ID would be able to learn that person's phone number, sex, and what time of day they're likely to be home. In this way, Caller ID coupled with Automatic Call Return allows the determined harasser to select the best prospects for abuse.

The per-call alternative shifts the burden of protecting privacy to the caller, after we have come to rely on a telephone system in which for the past 50 years the caller had a legitimate expectation of privacy. Shouldn't the party disturbing the privacy status quo — the phone companies — bear that burden?

Providing free per-line blocking lessens the burden on the calling party — there is no need to make a decision and to dial additional numbers with each outgoing call. It preserves choice for each telephone subscriber. It eliminates the threat of telemarketing abuses. It provides limited protection against redlining and against the loss of anonymity in calling hotlines or in dealing with domestic crises.

But it is important to remember that the protections are incomplete: Unscrupulous businesses could still choose not to service calls from certain neighborhoods AND calls whose numbers are blocked. This would put privacy-conscious callers at a disadvantage.

Callers would still have a perception of a loss of confidentiality when they call crisis hotlines, especially from the premises of an acquaintance. How do they know whether a friend's line has per-call or per-line blocking or no blocking *without revealing that they wish to make an anonymous call?*

What happens when you subscribe to per-line blocking and your friend or relative with Caller ID won't answer your call unless the incoming number is displayed? There is the concept of "call unblocking," which allows a caller with per-line blocking to "unblock" the blocking by pressing *67 or a similar code.

Telephone service is getting more complex, if nothing else, with the arrival of Caller ID.

Either way, with or without blocking or unblocking, Caller ID diminishes the perception of privacy and anonymity among all telephone users.

Permitting a service that displays only the *name,* not the number, of the calling phone overcomes many of the objections to number identification. Northern Telecom has developed the technology to deliver the name of the telephone subscriber, not the number. In a market trial in Boise, Idaho, 70,000 US West customers were able to get the *name* of the subscriber from whose phone the call originated. Customers liked it.

This is logical. People remember names, not digits. Telephone courtesy is to provide your name, not your number, when you place a call. Names cannot readily be used to trace the whereabouts of people, unlike numbers. Names can just as easily be used by companies to retrieve customer information, yet displaying names does not raise the same fears about secondary telemarketing uses.

The telephone companies' Call Trace and Distinctive Ringing features provide excellent protection from harassing calls, without the attendant negative consequences of Caller ID. Distinctive Ringing permits you to program your telephone so that when friends call you will hear a ring, but when strangers call you will hear a different ring or a buzzing. You can then decide whether you want to answer the phone. Telephone sets now sold in stores permit this capability without the need to subscribe to any additional telephone company service.

Customers in Rochester, New York, in a test, found Call Trace more effective than Caller ID in stopping harassing calls. Most customers used call blocking improperly or were unaware they had paid for it.

A nationwide survey conducted by Louis Harris and Associates found that 55 percent of persons surveyed wanted Caller ID regulated and 25 percent wanted it banned outright. Forty-eight percent would allow Caller ID only with call-blocking. Still, a quarter of the respondents thought Caller ID should be banned even if blocking is offered.

"Women, who it was thought would more strongly favor Caller ID than men because of its potential for screening potentially harassing phone calls, are considerably less likely than men to think Caller ID should be allowed," Harris reported. Strangely, the Harris organization decided to ask its questions a second time, this time stressing that Caller ID could deter harassing calls. This time there was only a six percent increase in the number favoring Caller ID without limitations. What's the conclusion?

Caller ID is a close call; its privacy implications go both ways.

This was weighed by the former Privacy Commissioner of Canada, John W. Grace, who addressed Caller ID in his annual report of 1989-90. The office of Privacy Commissioner was established in Canada to monitor privacy protections for its citizens. In contrast to the state-by-state approval process in the U.S., in Canada, Caller ID was approved at the federal level, by the Canadian Radio-Television and Telecommunications Commission (CRTC). Some Canadians now say that it was summarily approved before many of the drawbacks of the service discovered in the regulatory process in the U.S. became known in Canada. In fact, two years after giving an okay to Caller ID, the CRTC ordered Bell Canada to provide free blocking from now on.

Back in 1990, John Grace considered Caller ID and concluded,

"After some initial hesitation — one is reluctant to prescribe which privacy value is more important — the Commissioner concluded that the privacy minus outweighs the plus. At base, it is unacceptable that we should surrender our anonymity as a necessary condition of using the telephone.

"It would too greatly diminish the state of our personal privacy if every call we made to merchants, government departments, social agencies or media outlets disclosed our identities. To prevent that loss of control surely we are willing to tolerate the fact that some may abuse their ability to call anonymously."

Chapter Six
Birds Of A Feather
Into Sitting Ducks

Caller ID and Automatic Number Identification are only a small part of the technological advances permitting creative new ways of intrusive marketing.

Have you heard about "target marketing"? Some call it "database marketing"; others call it "targeting by taste." Whatever it's called, there is a startling change taking place in the way wholesalers and retailers try to get their products in the hands of consumers.

No longer are they content to advertise in mass media — spending millions of dollars for messages that may fall on deaf ears — and hope that customers will find their way to stores where thousands of items are displayed. Manufacturers and many retail outlets now want to target customers directly and lock them into consistent buying patterns.

The way to do this, of course, is to use precise lists for mail or telephone solicitation or to identify customers loyal to your brand and somehow manipulate them into buying your products over and over. The only way to accomplish this successfully is to know everything possible about your customers: their age, income, ethnicity, family size, credit cards, and buying habits.

Some target marketers, like Quaker Oats Co., want to know their customers' political and social views. In one massive direct-marketing campaign, Quaker Oats asked customers, including many children, their views on drug testing, school prayer, and gun control, on the theory that their responses indicate whether they are traditionalist or are open to new ideas. Kids and adults who ordered the Cap'n Crunch Dick Tracy Wrist Watch Radio through a Quaker Oats offer in cereal boxes were sent an intrusive questionnaire that asked about these three political issues, plus street address, income, what credit cards the family uses, the names, ages, and preferences of smokers in the household, and who has what diseases in the family. It also asked the wrist-watch radio users to agree or disagree strongly or moderately with the statement: "My dog is like my baby."

The company used the data to market other products directly to the family, based on its preferences. It then tracked the purchases so that it could reinforce patterns by marketing the identical products and allied products in the future. Customers will receive different levels of discounts depending on their family characteristics. Quaker Oats planned to "overlay" television, radio, and newspaper advertising and monitor the varying responses, thus completing the manipulation of the buyer.

When women reach the cash register at Casual Corner or August Max clothing stores, the clerks ask them for their telephone numbers and then enter the numbers into the cash register. We are conditioned to provide information like this innocently, because we have been led to believe that the merchant needs it to track us down if a check bounces or if a credit-card transaction is erroneous or invalid.

But the stores have other uses in mind for the information. They are gathering phone numbers from cash customers as well. The stores are using new computer software called REACT, which links the phone number with the customer's identity and address, age and income brackets, dwelling type, and previous purchases in the store. All of this has been stored in the retailers' in-house computer system — on 55 million persons.

Combining this information with a description of the current purchases permits the stores to court customers by mail, by telephone, or in the store for purchases for which the customer is known to be vulnerable. The computerized tracking system — called REACT — "allows retailers to turn every single customer into a loyal customer," according to Direct Marketing Technology in Schaumburg, Illinois, and Retail Consumer Technology in Connecticut, which developed it for $15 million. One of REACT's officers used the term "targeting by taste."

The REACT people stress that information is kept confidential by the stores and that providing the telephone number is purely voluntary. A customer is told, they say, that the phone number is requested for marketing purposes. No privacy threat.

But is that the end of the debate?

There are no prohibitions against Casual Corner or August Max peddling that personal information to other "target marketers." Nor is it correct to imply that customers know the consequences of providing a phone number when they do so innocently at the point of purchase.

It is a myopic view of privacy to say that so long as information is protected, the individual's privacy is protected. Privacy, in the 1990s, includes not only the right to control personal information about oneself and how it is used, but also the right to be free of manipulation, whether in the marketplace or vis-a-vis the government. Privacy includes the right to exercise autonomy in one's life and one's personal affairs.

Too often, when the trade press describes these retailing innovations, it includes the obligatory line, "Privacy advocates are concerned about the implications of the new technique." And that is the end of the analysis.

By the same token, in testifying before Congress in May 1990 on innovative target marketing by Citicorp Point-of-Sale Information Services, its president, Jerry Saltzgaber, said, "The answer to privacy concerns is *not* to prohibit or restrict the collection, access or use of personal information by marketers. Instead, consumers should be given, as we have already done, adequate disclosure of the uses of such information and provided with the capability to 'opt-out' by denying the use of personal information for unauthorized purposes."

Saltzgaber also proclaimed, "The time when manufacturers could market one product to all of us using mass market media is gone. The future of marketing is based on *actual* household purchases. With advancing technology, retailers and marketers can learn the preferences of their customer households, and then have the ability to give each household the product it wants."

Saltzgaber's use of the verb "give" was curious, and his declaration of victory over mass marketing was premature. It came just six months before Citicorp POS was forced to shut down a large part of its operation and let 174 of its 450 employees go. Saltzgaber found himself looking for other work. Citicorp POS abandoned a test called "Reward America," in which customers of the Ukrops supermarket chain in Richmond, Virginia, received discounts (in the form of "electronic coupons" credited at the point-of-sale) in exchange for permitting Citicorp to monitor each of their purchases and sell back the data in aggregate to merchants.

The Citicorp subsidiary will continue its other target programs, including those that track supermarket purchases with magazine readership, identify "lapsed shoppers," and segment customers into groups of coupon-sensitive buyers, new-product triers, price-sensitive shoppers, health-conscious shoppers, and long-time brand-loyalists.

The Uniform Product Code, placed on groceries to activate cash registers and to track inventory, is the key to many of these Orwellian innovations. Remember that the UPC appears on drugs, books and periodicals, personal-hygiene products, beverages, condoms, diapers, and any number of other products that provide telltale traces of our lifestyle choices.

Our traditional assumption that we may purchase these products anonymously is being lost.

Two separate ventures with the unfortunate names of ScanAmerica (part of Time Inc. and Arbitron) and Behaviorscan (a Chicago operation) track the purchases of volunteer families through the UPC. Behaviorscan goes one step further, altering the television commercials that each family receives over cable and then tracking the responses as soon as the family goes shopping.

The tracking technology goes much further than anything we had anticipated and so do the privacy concerns. While the technological marvels receive the attention when the products are unveiled, the privacy concerns get no more than a fleeting glance.

The very real threats to privacy can be seen best when highlighted against an unholy alliance formed in 1990 by Equifax Inc., the largest credit bureau/consumer reporting company in the U.S., and Lotus Development Co., maker of advanced software. Equifax and Lotus planned to launch "Lotus Market-Place: Households," a computer compact disk, read-only-memory (CD-ROM) containing demographic data on 80 million households. The disk would have been available to anyone who uses an Apple personal computer. The database would have included name, address, age range, sex, marital status, income bracket, dwelling type, shopping habits, and "products or lifestyle category."

Users could browse through the database, selecting demographic and consumer characteristics that fit their specialized needs, and then rent the names and addresses that fit their targets. Lotus calls this "desktop control."

What was shocking about this disk is that the source of the information was Equifax' millions of credit reports. Equifax was not extracting information about credit-worthiness or specific purchases from the credit-bureau database, as it is quick to point out. But the basic list of names was generated by credit files, as well as approximate data on credit-card usage, buying frequency, and types of purchase choices. Census information (not individually identifiable, but refined to

"Census blocks" of 200 or so persons) added to the demographic portraits.

Using techniques available elsewhere to identify its current clientele, a small business could have prowled through "MarketPlace: Households" to find more customers who are similarly situated. (As one target marketer told his open-mouthed colleagues, "We take 'birds of a feather' and make them 'sitting ducks.'")

Privacy advocates and computer professionals objected vigorously to the scheme, saying it represented "a quantum leap" in the dissemination of personal information for marketing. They generated 30,000 complaints to Lotus, an astounding number even considering the ease with which many of them generated the complaints by electronic mail and computer modem.

Because of this, Lotus and Equifax announced in January of 1991 that they were canceling sales of the disk. "The cost and complexity of educating consumers about the issue is beyond the scope of Lotus," said Jim Manzi, Lotus president, in announcing the reversal. "Lotus cannot afford a prolonged battle over consumer privacy." He called the opposition "an emotional fire storm."

Throughout the "fire storm," Equifax, which operates one of the nation's two largest nationwide credit bureaus, said that it was not using individual credit information for the "MarketPlace" disk. But in its advertising to the trade, Equifax says, at one point, "Lists include data from credit files as well," and at another point, "[Our lists are] based on financial, credit, and public record information." And Equifax Vice President John A. Baker betrayed more than he intended in January of 1991 by writing, "We provide opt-out capability to anyone who notifies us that they want their name removed from any *credit* or direct marketing lists sold."

Its major competitor in this massive transfer of credit-bureau information to the marketing business, TRW Information Services, claims in its trade advertising that its lists will describe a random consumer: "Bill Hayes is 32 years old, makes over $40,000 a year, uses his credit cards, and just moved to Florida because he loves to scuba dive... The result is an in-depth profile of your customer's buying habits, product needs, financial lifestyle and history."

Credit files are a notoriously inaccurate source for any kind of information. The companies themselves report that fully one-third of the people who examine their own records, as permitted by federal law, find errors!

The intent of the Fair Credit Reporting Act, when it was enacted in 1971, was to confine the use of information in credit reports to determining eligibility for credit, insurance, or employment. The Federal Trade Commission, which enforces the FCRA, said at one time that extracting *any information* from a credit file, even if just name and address, is the same as disclosing a full-dress credit report and triggers all of the consumer protections of the act, but Equifax and TRW ignored this.

The fair credit act reflects principles of "Fair Information Practices" carefully devised in the 1970s by a task force of the Department of Health, Education, and Welfare, by a respected IBM study, by the drafters of the 1974 federal Privacy Act, and by study commissions in Europe. The most important provision in the Code of Fair Information Practices is:

"Personal information gathered for one purpose (in this case credit) ought not to be used for another purpose (marketing), without the express consent of the individual."

This is fundamental fairness, but there's a practical reason for the principle. Incidental information when gathered originally, is rarely checked for accuracy, but may take on monumental significance when used in a totally different context much later. For example, most people don't care whether their age is accurate on a credit application, but if that information is used to determine insurance premiums it takes on new importance. If the individual has a chance to provide or withhold consent when information is to be disclosed, he or she becomes the best check for accuracy.

TRW and Equifax have repeatedly said they abide by this code. But both Equifax and TRW omit this key principle from the Fair Information Practices principles they distribute publicly.

Beyond that, the CD-ROM offering by Equifax and Lotus would have violated a principle of the right to privacy that has been recognized in American law since 1902. It has been called "the right of publicity." University of San Francisco trademarks expert J. Thomas McCarthy has written, quite simply:

"The Right of Publicity is the right of a person to control the commercial use of his or her identity."[1]

The preeminent authority on the law of torts, William L. Prosser, in 1960 labeled this personal tort "appropriation" and applied it to the commercial use of one's likeness, name, or facts about his or her persona, for someone else's profit.[2] It creates, "in effect, for every individual, a common law trade name, his own, and a common law trade mark in his likeness...much

---

[1] J. Thomas McCarthy, *The Rights of Publicity and Privacy* (Clark Boardman, 1987).

[2] William L. Prosser, "Privacy," 48 *California Law Review* 383 (1960).

more extensive than those which any corporation...can expect."

Most privacy scholars have said that the rationale for protecting this right is to prevent "rip-offs," the unjust enrichment of a corporation by misappropriating the property of another, his or her name or face. But one, Edward G. Bloustein, the late President of Rutgers University, has argued that what is being prohibited by this principle of law is "a wrongful exercise of dominion over another... The wrong involved is the objective diminution of personal freedom rather than the infliction of personal suffering or the misappropriation of property." At any rate, most states have come to recognize this right in the years since New York first enacted explicit protection in 1903.

To date, courts have turned to the "right to publicity" mainly in cases involving the use of a name or likeness, without consent, in advertising, especially when an endorsement is implied. No court has been willing to apply the rule to the use of a name in a commercial mailing list. The invasion of privacy has been regarded as slight; "the walk from the mail slot to the trash can is a short one," wrote one judge.

But that attitude of courts may change in the 1990s. Target marketing creates a whole new dimension of misappropriation. What is being disclosed here is not merely one's name, but also revealing information about how one spends his or her money and, consequently, how one conducts his or her life. This commercial use entitles the individual to compensation.

Rather than exposing a person to a one-time use of the name and address (for which the damages are no more than a dime or a quarter in the current market), ventures like Lotus MarketPlace exploit the person's name *for an unlimited number of uses,* by an unlimited number of personal-computer users, many of whom have no moral compunctions about using their cyber-imaginations to play dirty tricks.

It is this vulnerability that elevated the Equifax-Lotus product to an extreme privacy threat: Individual data would have been in the hands not merely of businesses subject to federal, state, and local regulatory schemes and to public scrutiny *but also to any computer user who could purchase an Apple computer and the $695 retail price of the software.*

We should know from experience that unwanted mail is not the only harm that can result. There have been several cases of men consulting a database — the public listings of registered drivers in each state motor vehicle department — to stalk young women. The man who was obsessed with TV actress Rebecca Schaeffer in 1989 learned of her home address through California's motor vehicle records. Six weeks later, the man shot Rebecca Schaeffer to death outside of her Los Angeles apartment. The people at Lotus call this example "unnecessarily inflammatory."

Is it safe to make millions of home addresses — and indirectly millions of listed and unlisted home telephone numbers — available to anonymous individuals tapping on their keyboards in their bedrooms?

What is to be done?

The Federal Trade Commission and Congress must make sure that the limits of the Fair Credit Reporting Act are obeyed. Information gathered for credit purposes ought to be used only for that purpose, unless the individual consents otherwise.

The target marketing companies, including the marketing divisions of the major credit bureaus, must refrain from offering over-the-counter packages of personal information, unless they compensate the persons who are listed. Equifax, for its part, not only shut down the Lotus venture but also voluntarily quit using information from its credit-bureau files as a source for its marketing lists.

Customers must insist upon shopping in the old-fashioned way: leaving absolutely no "paper trail," by paying with cash.

If they use credit cards, they should provide no information beyond a signature. Upon getting authorization, the merchant is assured of payment and needs no telephone numbers, addresses, nor Social Security numbers.

If they pay by check, conversely, consumers should present valid identification, but refuse to provide credit cards and especially refuse to permit merchants to put Social Security numbers or credit-card numbers on the checks.

Consumers should fill out credit applications judiciously. This will deny merchants and marketers much of the grist for their manipulative mills.

In the end, the *segmentation* of America belittles us all. It is not the best use of our talents and resources, including our computer technology, to package people in little boxes so that we may sell them more products they don't need. Why is it that computers are used for the most trivial of our pursuits?

Just as gossip journalism demeans and cheapens public figures and drags the rest of us down to a level of Peeping Toms, target marketing lessens all of us by peddling our personal information without our permission and by manipulating our personal choices in the marketplace. That, more than any breach of confidentiality, is the invasion of our privacy.

Chapter Seven
Medical Information
Is Confidential, But...

In recognizing a *constitutional right to privacy,* the U.S. Supreme Court has more than once said that at the core of this right is control over one's body and, with that, an expectation of confidentiality in medical treatment. In the 1973 case upholding the right to an abortion, *Roe v. Wade,* the majority opinion cited one of the earliest recognitions of a "right to be let alone," a case upholding the refusal of a plaintiff in a lawsuit to be compelled to submit to an involuntary medical exam.[1]

In a companion case to *Roe,* Justice William O. Douglas wrote, "The right to privacy has no more con-

---

[1] *Union Pacific Railway Co. v. Botsford,* 141 U.S. 250 (1891).

spicuous place than in the physician-patient relationship unless it be in the priest-penitent relationship.
The right to seek advice on one's health and the right
to place reliance on the physician of one's choice are
basic to Fourteenth Amendment values."[2]

This "right" often seems more rhetorical than actual. There are many occasions when one's medical
history is not confidential. This is especially true in an
era when virtually all payments for medical treatment
are handled by a third party, whether a private insurer or a governmental insurer.

In other words, the rhetoric among judges about
the sanctity of medical confidentiality is overshadowed
by the reality that medical information is freely available to insurance companies, employers, and consumer
reporting agencies (because of the freely worded
authorization patients sign) or available to others
(because of carelessness or deception).

For instance, the public is entitled to an
individual's mental health records held by a public
agency if the need is compelling enough, according to
the West Virginia Supreme Court. Worried parents
had tried to compel a school superintendent to release
the full mental record of a school bus driver who
related mystical and occult thoughts to his young
passengers. One's right to privacy is outweighed if
disclosure does not create a substantial intrusion, if
the public interest is significant, if the information is
unavailable elsewhere, if there was no expectation of
confidentiality when the information was provided,
and if the invasion of privacy can be limited, the court
said.[3]

---

[2] *Doe v. Bolton*, 410 U.S. 179 (1973).
[3] *Child Protection Group v. Cline*, 350 SE 2d 541 (1986).

Similarly, the Massachusetts Supreme Judicial Court ordered a psychiatrist to turn over to a grand jury his patient records and diagnoses. The grand jury was investigating Medicaid fraud. At least 27 of the psychiatrist's patients had objected to the disclosure. The court, however, limited its order to records that were necessary to the investigation and excluded the doctor's notes of what patients said in therapy sessions. The court implied that a higher standard of confidentiality protects psychotherapy records. "Records... which reflect patients' thoughts, feelings, and impressions... are protected and need not be produced."[4]

Among the four recognized aspects of the privacy tort — (1) intrusion into one's solitude; (2) casting a person in a false light (even though the information is technically true); (3) misappropriating a person's likeness or persona for a commercial purpose; and (4) public disclosure of private facts (even though the information is true) — it is the fourth that most often arises in a medical context.

An example of the disclosure of private facts is a 1990 case in Massachusetts in which a physician notified a newspaper of a woman's medical condition. After arranging for midwives to deliver her baby at home, a woman developed complications and was rushed to a hospital. She was prepared for an emergency cesarean delivery while, according to the woman, a doctor lectured her on the dangers of home delivery. The baby died. The physician's partner, without witnessing the birth or consulting with the attending physician or speaking with the mother, called the local newspaper. Both doctors described the details of the delivery to the press. The paper did not disclose her name, but the woman said that people in the community could rec-

---

[4] *Commonwealth v. Kobrin*, 395 Mass. 284 (1985).

ognize her identity in the newspaper's article. She sued for invasion of privacy and a related tort, intentional infliction of emotional distress. The jury awarded her damages on both counts.[5]

All states but Rhode Island, South Carolina, Texas, and Vermont recognize a "doctor-patient" privilege. That means that doctors may not be compelled to testify in court about medical facts received in confidence. The privilege does not directly affect disclosures voluntarily made by a physician or those made out of court. Nor does it necessarily protect medical information in the hands of non-professionals.

Doctors are also bound by ethical restrictions on patient confidentiality, stemming from the ancient oath of Hippocrates, the Greek physician regarded as a father of medicine. The rationale of this code — that total candor is essential for quality medical care — was articulated best by a federal court in Ohio, in 1965:

"Since the layman is unfamiliar with the road to recovery, he cannot sift the circumstances of his life and habits to determine what is information pertinent to his health. As a consequence, he must disclose all information... even that which is disgraceful or incriminating. To promote full disclosure, the medical profession extends the promise of secrecy... The candor which this promise elicits is necessary to the effective pursuit of health; there can be no reticence, no reservations, no reluctance..."[6]

A very few states — notably California, Colorado, Illinois, and Rhode Island — have sought to codify doc-

---

[5] *Becker v. Topal,* CA 88-354 (Mass. Super. Ct., Hampshire Co., Sept. 20, 1990), *Privacy Journal* May 1991.
[6] *Hammonds v. Aetna Casualty & Surety Co.,* 243 F. Supp. 793 (N.D. Ohio 1965).

tor-patient confidentiality with laws requiring medical information to be kept confidential.

In those states where there is no statute, courts have declared that there exists a *fiduciary duty* on the part of medical professionals to keep patient information confidential. For instance, the Supreme Court of Alabama has stated, "It must be concluded that a medical doctor is under a general duty not to make extra-judicial disclosures of information acquired in the course of the doctor-patient relationship and that a breach of that duty will give rise to a cause of action. It is, of course, recognized that this duty is subject to exceptions prompted by the supervening interests of society, as well as the private interests of the patient himself."[7] The court said further, "Unauthorized disclosure of intimate details of a patient's health may amount to unwarranted publicization of one's private affairs with which the public has no legitimate concern such as to cause outrage, mental suffering, shame or humiliation to a person of ordinary sensibilities. Nor can it be said that an employer is necessarily a person who has a legitimate interest in knowing each and every detail of an employee's health. Certainly, there are many ailments about which a patient might consult his private physician which have no bearing or effect on one's employment."

Similarly, the Supreme Court of South Dakota, where there is a law requiring patient confidentiality, said that a psychiatrist was wrong to provide information on a patient in a post-divorce custody action.

An important exception to the general rule of non-disclosure is an instance when a professional is obli-

---

[7] *Horne v. Patton*, 291 Ala. 701, 287, So. 2d 824 (1973).

gated to prevent harm to another and *should* therefore release information gained in a patient consultation.[8]

The AIDS epidemic has created special concerns about the disclosure of individual medical information because of the stigma the disease seems to have. Disclosure of the results of an individual's HIV test or of the status of a person with AIDS is prohibited by many state laws passed in the last seven years.

In the past five years, courts have held that disclosure of information about AIDS is an invasion of privacy, whether or not a law is on the books.

In New Jersey, a policeman learned that a man had AIDS and notified neighbors, who in turn removed their children from the school that the patient's children attended. "The Constitution protects the family from governmental disclosure of the husband's infection with the virus," a federal court ruled. "Disclosure of a family member's medical condition, especially exposure to or infection with the AIDS virus, is a disclosure 'of a personal nature.' "

A California court has ruled that the explicit right to privacy in the state constitution protects against disclosure of a man's HIV status to an employer. The man was fired.

But, a doctor's testing of a couple for the HIV virus, without consent, as part of a pre-marital blood screening did not fit into the four traditional branches of the common-law tort of invasion of privacy. No disclosure of the results was made beyond the couple's medical file, according to the highest court in Pennsylvania.

---

[8] *Tarasoff v. Regents*, 13 Cal. 3d 177, 118 Cal. Rptr. 129, 529 P. 2d 553 (Cal. 1974).

For an individual to sustain a right of action, it is important, but not absolute, that the person have "an expectation of privacy." Thus, when a company adopts internal rules protecting the confidentiality of employee information, this fortifies an employee's expectation of privacy, according to the U.S. First Circuit Court of Appeals. It ruled in favor of an IBM employee who claimed an invasion of privacy when company doctors discussed his mental condition with managers.[9]

An absolute defense to a common-law claim of privacy invasion is that the victim *consented.* In a medical context, a knowing, informed authorization to release medical data serves this purpose. This means that the language and the circumstances of an authorization form that a patient is asked to sign are crucial. Patients should be sure to alter the language of the authorization so that it permits limited release of medical information concerning only the current treatment, that it lists the professionals and/or organizations to which disclosure may be made, that the authorization has an expiration date, and that language saying that a photocopy is as valid as the original is eliminated.

But where is the consent when patient information is used for marketing purposes? Patients are shocked to discover that information about their medical conditions is finding its way into the marketing network.

Many doctors' offices have agreed to let information companies tap into their computer records about patients, according to a front-page story in *The Wall Street Journal.* These companies are interested in the kinds of drugs and the amounts of drugs that are being prescribed so that they can market that information to manufacturers and retailers. The companies tell the

---

[9] *Bratt v. IBM Corp.,* 785 F 2d 352 (1st Cir. 1986).

doctors that they are not interested in the identities of the patients. But how can doctors be sure?

There are no assurances that patient identities will not be disclosed, either intentionally or accidentally.

Other information companies are tapping into the computers used by pharmacies to keep track of each customer's purchases and dosages. Only a few pharmacists are refusing to go along; only a few showed that they respect patients' expectations of confidentiality.

Hospitals, too, are using patient information in their marketing operations.

You know when they advertise free prostate screening or skin-cancer screening or when they set up free blood pressure or obesity checks in the shopping malls? When you provide your name and address, hospitals and clinics are using this information to market services to you — the same way Publishers Clearinghouse sells magazines or J.C. Penney sells life insurance.

If a test shows you have high cholesterol or shortness of breath, you can expect to be deluged with mail and phone calls from the hospital promoting its services.

"The basic idea is to segment consumers in the hospital's service area by health problem and then sell them hospital services and procedures to combat that problem," reported *Modern Healthcare* magazine. Will they be renting or exchanging lists next?

Is this fair? Is it responsible for providers of health care to do this?

With more assertiveness by patients, the very high expectation we have of the confidentiality of medical information may someday be matched by actual practices in the health field.

Chapter Eight
Testing: One, Two, Three

Recognition of medical confidentiality is crucial because medical information is now in the hands of the entity that controls our ability to make a living — our employer.

Employers also collect and keep on file a lot of information that passes for medical information. It is based on various tests that are administered when we apply for a job or after we are on the job.

In this age of high tech, employers are increasingly relying on some rather low-tech, and often unreliable, methods for selecting employees.

They seem no longer interested in experience, skills, and character to determine whether an individual is qualified for a particular job. Instead they have delegated the task of screening applicants to impersonal measurements — urinalysis, blood tests, fingerprints, psychological tests, "pen-and-pencil honesty tests," computerized criminal-record checks, and even handwriting and astrology.

Each of these methods has what many people in the high-tech era consider a benefit: the tests avoid the necessity to confront other people directly.

This has profound implications for the individuality, dignity, and privacy of employees in America.

"We are frisking each other," *New York Times* columnist William Safire once wrote. "Picture yourself going to work tomorrow, handing over blood and urine samples, taking a quick turn with the house polygraph, turning out your pockets and walking through some new fluoroscope. You object? Whatsamatter, you got something to hide?"

Each of these methods has different levels of reliability and intrusiveness (and legality), and so employers and employees have to be discriminating. Applicants must know the attributes of each screening device and decide whether the job is worth the indignity.

The most fraudulent of these devices is the polygraph, or so-called lie detector. Federal law now virtually bans the devices for screening applicants.

The current fad — and that is what it is — is the use of urinalysis tests to detect the presence of drugs. The sudden popularity of this methodology in the early 1980s was due directly to a test developed and aggressively marketed by the Syva Corp. in California. The test is simple and cheap. It produced what seemed to be a perfect weapon in the war on drugs: a way to determine the presence of drugs by analyzing a person's urine.

The trouble is that it also picks up the presence of substances besides illegal drugs, like aspirin, codeine, or herbal diet products. It does not distinguish between one-time use and habitual abuse. (In fact, there is medical evidence that the Syva test is *more likely* to pick up the one-time user, not the addict.) Nor does the test measure impairment on the job, only the possible presence of drugs within the past several days. The manufacturers warn that the test is not valid without a confirming test using a different methodology, but many employers and laboratories ignore this. A judge in Massachusetts, citing expert testimony, concluded flatly that Syva's test "is never conclusive."

Unlike the case of the polygraph, there seem to be alternative methods of analyzing urine that have a higher reliability rate than the readily available Syva product. But these alternatives are expensive and, except in major league baseball, not often used by employers. Commonly, applicants and employees are simply rejected or disciplined on the basis of the once-over-lightly Syva test or its clones.

Here the development of the polygraph is instructive. It was developed as a means of measuring *stress* in highly structured interrogations; it was never intended as an absolute indicator of truth or falsity, especially in the hands of inexperienced examiners. The Syva urinalysis test was intended to measure marijuana use in large groups. It was never thought to be precise enough to determine the fate of one individual.

Whereas the polygraph was favored by small, often shaky businesses, the urinalysis test is favored by large corporations and shunned by small operations. Nearly a fifth of Fortune's 500 largest corporations reported using drug testing in the mid-1980s.

There is new evidence that use of the tests has peaked. A 1991 study by the U.S. Department of Labor found that one out of three companies that had urinalysis tests in 1988 had discontinued them by 1990. It was mostly companies with fewer than 50 employees that were discovering that urinalysis programs were not worthwhile. Large companies were continuing their programs largely because federal law required them to do so in order to continue to do federal contract work. A study in the *Journal of the American Medical Association* at the same time showed that drug testing is not cost effective unless drug use in the workplace is known to be high.

A leading laboratory involved in this distasteful work, SmithKline-Beecham, reported fewer and fewer positive test results in the past five years. In federal agencies and in college athletics, drug testing has succeeded only in showing that drug use there is miniscule (one half of one percent). Was this because the threat or reality of drug testing has successfully deterred drug use, or was it because drug use was never a major problem in most workplaces in the first place?

While the fad was hot, 13 states moved to restrict it: California, Florida, Hawaii, Iowa, Maine, Maryland, Minnesota, Montana, Nebraska, New Mexico, Oregon, Rhode Island, and Vermont.

We can now see that during the drug-testing mania many people got hurt. Their dignity, their self-esteem was irreparably damaged.

For instance:

A flight attendant in California suffered medical complications because of federal transportation requirements that compel drug-testing monitors to have employees drink water until they can provide a urine sample. The 40-year-old woman was pressured to drink more and more water — three quarts of it — and expected to urinate in a crowded room. She couldn't. After three hours she was sent home. That night she couldn't sleep and she couldn't urinate. She was hospitalized with water intoxification.

A husky oil rig worker was so humiliated about having to urinate in front of co-workers that he began to weep when testifying about it before a jury. He was awarded compensatory damages in his lawsuit.

A woman employed at a nuclear plant in Georgia described her experience: "The first day I went in I could not give enough urine. The second day, the nurse made me stand in the middle of the bathroom with one hand in the air, with my pants around my ankles, and a bottle between my legs. She walked real close behind me and leaned over. I was scared she was going to touch me. She screamed at me that I had not followed procedure, and I was going to have to do it again. Well, needless to say, I did not do it again, and I will never, if it means that I will never have a job again, I will never do that again."

Yet most Americans supported drug testing in the workplace and still do. Isn't this based on their misunderstanding of the actual humiliation involved in the process, on their misguided faith in the reliability of the methodology, on their abhorrence of drug use at work, and on their fear of being suspected of being tolerant of drug use? This is reminiscent of the McCarthyism era in the 1950s, another time when Americans abandoned their good judgment and accepted a cure worse than the disease.

The blood test for the HIV virus, like nearly all tests, is not 100-percent reliable. There are many "false positives" in any test. These are results that falsely show the presence of the virus. Any test also produces the opposite effect, "false negatives." And it is important to remember that a confirmed positive test will show that the individual has the virus, not the AIDS condition itself. Still, the HIV test, when confirmed, is reliable enough for its purposes, to advise individuals of their health condition.

But, in view of the Public Health Service's unequivocal advisory that AIDS is not transmitted by other than sexual contact or blood transference, is there any rationale for employers to require AIDS tests of applicants or employees? Most employers at present have answered no.

The states of Montana, Nebraska, New Mexico, Vermont, Washington, and Wisconsin ban AIDS testing in the workplace. Most states prohibit AIDS testing without consent.

Some companies have begun testing applicants' and employees' blood for the presence of genetic traits that are said to make one susceptible to certain substances in the workplace or to have a likelihood of developing certain inherited diseases. Genetic screening will detect certain diseases that are inherited or a susceptibility to certain diseases that are not directly inherited. For example, a certain gene seems to show a propensity for Alzheimer's disease, but not a direct inheritance of the disease; not everyone with the gene seems to get Alzheimer's disease.

Genetic screening can also expose vulnerabilities to certain environmental exposures. For example, some people with a particular gene that results in a deficiency of an enzyme may face a destruction of their red blood cells if they take an anti-malarial drug. Some scientists believe that there are many substances used in manufacturing that have properties similar to the anti-malarial drug. People identified with this condition, therefore, should be warned against exposure to these substances on the job.

At present, according to the Congressional Office of Technology Assessment, "The power to identify biological risks (that is, the exposure to infectious disease or genetic vulnerability to chemicals in the environment) often outstrips the capability to remove or reduce those risks. This raises a demand for social control measures that sometimes impinge on constitutional freedoms."

During this interim period when there is a gap between our ability to identify genetic conditions and our inability to do much about them, is it fair to deprive a person of making a living based on genetic screening? And is it any business of an employer to know sensitive medical conditions that the individual himself or herself may not be aware of yet and that may have no effect on one's ability to do a job? Wisconsin has moved to regulate genetic testing, but no other state has yet.

With benign motives, employers could use test results to assign employees to safe environments and to warn them of risks, not to bar them from jobs.

The danger is that this new DNA technology will be used in unsophisticated ways in the workplace, just as polygraphs, urinalysis, and other developments have been. It could be used as an absolute denial of employment, rather than a red flag or a guide to safe assignments. It could be used merely to reject applicants who may cause concern to the employer's health-insurance provider. Used as a shortcut to selecting employees, DNA screening will be disastrous for many innocent people.

Now that polygraph testing is prohibited, some companies use "pen-and-pencil honesty tests," designed to elicit responses that betray a dishonest personality. The problem for the job applicant is that no one knows the "right" answer to questions like, "Do most people steal?" or "Should a judge dismiss a minor stealing charge against a poor person?" That includes the authors of the "tests." They don't know the right answers either, but they purport to tell companies which employees will be trustworthy based on answers to these questions.

Many state laws prohibiting polygraphs in employment — including those in Connecticut, Maryland, Michigan, Minnesota, Nebraska, and Wisconsin — also prohibit honesty testing. Massachusetts and Rhode Island prohibit them explicitly.

No laws specifically address psychological tests in the workplace, although nearly every state human rights commission has declared that use of the most popular test violates state anti-discrimination requirements.

That test is the controversial Minnesota Multiphasic Personality Inventory.

Because of such attention to the MMPI, questions about sexual activities, religious beliefs, and bladder and bowel functions have been eliminated from a revised version.

The test is used regularly in the selection and assignment of employees. It had never been revised since it was first published in 1942. Think of the changes in the American workplace since then.

The old version of the Minnesota test asked job applicants for true or false responses to statements like these: "I have never had any black tarry-looking bowel movements." "I have never noticed any blood in my urine." "I pray several times a week." "Christ performed miracles." "I like mannish women." "I have diarrhea once a month or more." "My sex life is satisfactory."

Can you imagine job applicants sitting through this insulting exercise? No wonder they found the questions offensive. The authors of the test, who are affiliated with the University of Minnesota, admitted this.

It took them 37 years to figure that out.

The MMPI test has been the target of a lengthy class-action lawsuit for invasion of privacy and discrimination, filed in 1989 against Target Stores in California by an applicant for a security job.

The authors of the MMPI may have deleted some offensive questions, but they are still in the dark ages. To test the validity of their questions they go to rural Minnesota, somewhere just south of Lake Wobegon. Is this any way to determine whether a test has any relevance to the diverse American work force?

The authors have included some curious true-false queries in the revised test: "I am very seldom troubled by constipation." "I love my father." "I have never vomited or coughed up blood." "There is very little love and compassion in my home." "I like to talk about sex."

Here's another, to be answered true or false: "I have wished I were a girl. (Or if you are a girl) I have never been sorry that I am a girl."

It's hard to imagine that question getting by any enlightened state human rights commission — or past any self-respecting woman who is applying for work, and does not consider herself *a girl.*

It should be no surprise that some employers have resorted to more imaginative shortcuts, including using handwriting analysis to assign or evaluate applicants. It is astounding that sophisticated companies — the same companies that insist on detailed fact-finding before making a major marketing or investment decision — will rely on the unexamined views of a graphologist (some call themselves "graphoanalysts") in the crucial decisions about hiring employees.

A few companies, though not those in the terrestrial mainstream, rely on astrology for selecting and assigning employees.

A more serious threat to civil liberties is the federal government's push to require fingerprints and computerized criminal records checks of certain employees who work with children or the elderly — or who work with our apparently next-ranking national asset, nuclear power. The flaw in this effort is that, according to the federal government's own studies, the accuracy and timeliness of computerized criminal records are at an unacceptably low level. Beyond that, few child abusers or sex offenders are in these files; they are family members and friends who have not been prosecuted. (Nor do potential nuclear terrorists generally register with the police under their correct names and Social Security numbers.)

If a man can rise to become Secretary General of the United Nations with a sordid history of Nazi collaboration *on file,* how effective can we expect computerized criminal checks to be in purifying certain workplaces?

As in the case of testing applicants for drugs to keep addicts out of the workplace and demanding identity papers from applicants to confront the problem of undocumented aliens, we seem to impose restrictions on the law-abiding majority in our country rather than to target our efforts at the segment causing the problem we are trying to solve. The consequence is that the innocent majority is hampered by restrictions on their liberties with no apparent deterrent effect on crime or drug use or illegal immigration.

All of these high-tech shortcuts have lulled personnel executives and supervisors into a false sense of security. All of this is also intrusive and degrading to the individual. It has created a pool of workers who are intimidated and unsophisticated. No longer are close supervision, job-performance testing, and careful auditing valued highly by companies. The inclination is to hire the persons who survive the gauntlet of tests — and to assume that they are free from temptation and irresponsibility once they are on the job.

An employee with nothing to hide may well be an employee with nothing to offer.

In the 1990s, we seem to have developed a blind faith that objective measuring devices — preferably those that plug into an electrical socket and produce cathode-ray lettering — are less risky ways of selecting good people than are subjective human judgments.

A flat ban on all of these devices might be as unwise as an insistence that they all work equally well. Still, we can legislate that no person be deprived of employment solely for declining to submit to any of these tests. Informed experts are split on assessing the effectiveness of these methodologies; we should support the right of an employee or applicant to decline to have a crucial job decision based on them.

Chapter Nine
The Curse Of Robin Leach

At the same time that Americans are confronted with all sorts of high-tech threats to their privacy in their private lives, they are also enduring an onslaught of gossip journalism in both tabloids and the mainstream press.

The current spate of gossip journalism surely has been longer and much more intense than previous ones.

We can understand the reasons why by simply looking to the journalistic roots of the men and women who now own, manage, or edit most of the gossip media — both the electronic and the print varieties.

Most of them are British or Australian. There's the late Robert Maxwell, the Briton who owned the *Daily*

News in New York, and there's the 1980s owner of the major gossip competitor in the streets of New York, Australian Rubert Murdoch of the *New York Post.*

The supermarket tabloid *National Enquirer* is published by a Scotsman named Iain Calder. The area around Lantana, Florida, where the Enquirer is based, has become an expatriate haven for the top tabloid journalists from London. *National Enquirer, Globe, Sun,* and *Weekly World News* — all of them based in or around Lantana — are all written and edited mainly by British journalists.

It should not be a surprise that the new editor of *TV Guide* is a British expatriate; the "bible of television," after all, is a Murdoch-owned property. Anthea Disney reports that she learned her journalism at *The Daily Sketch,* one of London's tabloids. "It meant I could ask anybody anything and not be considered rude," she told the (currently) American-owned *New York Times.* After *The Daily Sketch*, Disney moved to Murdoch's *Daily News* and then became a TV producer at the Murdoch-owned Fox TV network. Her assignment: "Current Affair," the first show to bring the gossip and sensationalism tradition to television.

Did it all begin with Robin Leach, the groveling Australian who introduced to American television his breathless curiosity about the "Lifestyles of the Rich and Famous"?

Now *The New Yorker* magazine is in the hands of a Briton, the new editor Tina Brown. Before she had been on the job three months, spy-novelist John le Carre accused her of importing sleazy British journalistic tactics. Ms. Brown earned her reputation by "snazzing up" *Vanity Fair* magazine with what one journalist described as "crazed dictators, narcissistic movie stars, philandering politicians and pederastic priests."

Do Americans realize how alien all of this is to our culture? To be sure, we have had our gossip journalism in the past. But the mainstream press used to isolate the tabloids. When the daily press in 1992 picked up the story about Bill Clinton's extramarital affair, "news-gathering" by the tabloids became merged with mainstream journalism.

The British invented tabloid journalism at the turn of the century. They have mastered its niceties. By comparison, American journalists — even the ones who cover a Presidential campaign like a horse race — are viewed by the British as puritanical and deadly dull.

In England the policy makers and the literati may read the tabloids along with "the qualities" like *The Guardian* and *The Times,* but everybody knows that what's in the tabloids isn't to be taken seriously. But here in America the tabloids can affect an election, as we have seen. Americans seem more willing than Europeans to believe this stuff.

British journalists develop an obsession with ferreting out news about their royal family — an institution that seems to have been designed to foster snoopy, celebrity-fawning reporters. American journalists, by contrast, see the press as a vehicle for exposing corruption in high places and for sticking up for the little guy.

But there's a far more significant tradition the British invasion has brought to America. British journalists know nothing of our strong constitutional protection for freedom of the press. By comparison, American journalists grow up with our strong tradition of a free press. They know that they have to practice self-restraint and good judgment to have any credibility; the government isn't going to exercise that judgment for them.

"Great Britain has less freedom of expression than just about any democracy in the world," according to *Newsweek* in 1990. The Official Secrets Act still prevents disclosure of anything the government wants not to reveal; there are no limits on prior restraint of the press by the courts; the libel laws in England are much tougher for journalists.

When the British and Australians, talented as they are at celebrity reporting, come to America, they act like children at Halloween. They go wild — unrestricted by governmental censorship. They also discover as they gather stories something that the great French commentator Alexis de Tocqueville learned about us in the last century — that Americans are far more willing than Europeans to reveal intimate details.

This Anglicizing of the American press has created the current episode of trivialized news-gathering. It has permeated the rest of the print and electronic news media, which now have an obsession with the personal and the tawdry.

This means that the privacy of each of us is less secure, especially if we willingly or unwillingly become the subject of news coverage. A tragedy in the family, the witnessing of a crime, knowing someone else who becomes newsworthy, a happenstance in our lives — any of these events can thrust us into the spotlight and expose us to press coverage.

This fosters an environment in which invasions of privacy are not only tolerated, *they are desired.* This lowers the societal standards as to what constitutes an invasion of privacy. The legal protection, after all, is based on *expectations of privacy.*

News reporters who used to know better now assault us with outrageous inquiries — and select only the trivial, the intrusive, and the embarrassing from everything that we have said.

That is the cost to each of us as individuals because of the new tabloid "journalism."

This affects us all as consumers of news and entertainment; increasingly we are deprived of meaningful news that is relevant to our lives because it is obscured by all the gossip and titillation.

There is a cost as well to our society. The Anglicizing of the press merely enables American readers and viewers to avoid the realities in their own lives and the needs in their own localities. In the end it cheapens our culture.

Chapter Ten
What Rules For The Press?

It's usually difficult to persuade members of the press to abide by standards for fair conduct and fair reporting. Most reporters and editors see visions of censorship whenever it is suggested that standards should guide their work. Most are not very introspective about their work. Each decision is "a judgment call," determined by the serendipity of who's available at the time, not by a rational set of guidelines.

But average citizens who may find themselves thrust into newsworthy situations or whose careers or civic activities bring them into contact with the press are entitled to impose upon the press reasonable expectations when it comes to reporting on private lives.

And average citizens need to know what legal standards there are.

Perhaps by default, it has been left to a politician to come up with useful privacy guidelines for the press. Congressman Barney Frank, in 1988, shortly before his own personal life came to the attention of the news media, offered a set of "rules" that he thinks the national press and politicians have tacitly, and perhaps subconsciously, agreed upon. Before looking at that, let's review the current legal standards for invasion of privacy and then the author's suggestions for reasonable standards for journalists.

First, what is the law, as developed over the years by court cases involving the press?

1. Privacy protects only sensitive, personal information, not *all* information about a person. Even sensitive information may be published if it is newsworthy. Courts have said, however, that "a morbid and sensational prying into private lives for its own sake" is not protected by freedom of the press.

2. There can be no complaint about an invasion of privacy if a person has knowingly provided consent. But that consent may later be revoked if an individual discovers that the tone or context of a story is different from what was originally anticipated.

3. The passage of time may create a privacy right that did not exist when the information was current.

4. The privacy right diminishes, virtually to zero, at the time of death. Still, personal information about a deceased person may reflect on a living relative and therefore invade that person's privacy.

5. The right to privacy is uniquely a personal right. Organizations, like corporations and government agencies, do not have a right to privacy (even though they may have an interest in confidentiality at some times).

6. Intrusion upon one's solitude by the press and the publication of private facts cause real pain, often for a long period, and can threaten one's personal security.

7. There is an absolute right to publish, but no "right to know." There is an absolute right to publish, but no immunity from later consequences for something that was published. There is an absolute right to publish, but there is not always an absolute *need* to publish.

The author has added to this set of principles a few of his own. These have no legal effect at present but can serve as sensible standards for a news organization:

8. Just because information has been published one place (in a community newsletter or a tabloid paper) doesn't make it public property everywhere.

9. The more innocent the newsworthy behavior, the higher the entitlement to privacy protection. Having an illness is not evidence of wrongdoing and so the claim to privacy protection should be higher than in the case of sexual misconduct. By the same token, if the claim to privacy is high and the news-worthiness marginal, the privacy claim should prevail.

10. Family members did not sign on for the glare of publicity; they ought not be open targets for press coverage. Reporters and editors should give special consideration to publicity's impact on the children of people in the news.

11. When personal information is involved, reporters and editors should take extra time and care, even delaying a story if necessary to reexamine its accuracy, its newsworthiness, and its negative impact on the individuals involved.

12. Reporters should instinctively assume that any government document concerning an individual is inaccurate or misleading.

13. The ultimate question for a reporter is, "Would I deserve to live with the consequences if the information was published about me?"

Now let's turn to the "rules" that prevail in Washington, according to one of its survivors, Congressman Barney Frank of Massachusetts.[1]

1. For public officials, there is a right to privacy but not a right to hypocrisy. "The press should be hard on politicians who vote one way and conduct their lives in a different way," said Frank. "The people who make the rules should be subject to them," said Frank, quoting British philosopher John Locke. Under this rule, apparently, the press pursues reports of marital infidelity against politicians who claim to value their family lives or reports of homosexuality about a public figure who is anti-gay in public.

2. There are private activities that impair one's abilities, and these should be exposed. Frank was referring to abuse of alcohol or drugs or excessive sexual activities.

3. Public officials have a right to privacy, although one more diminished than the average citizen's. "The notion that you have no right to privacy because you are a public figure is nonsense," he said.

4. Activities that reflect negatively on one's character should be reported. "Does private activity show a rotten personality?" was Frank's standard. He said that abuse of a spouse is an example of private ac-

---

[1] In a speech at Central Connecticut State University April 9, 1988, reported in *Privacy Journal* April 1988.

tivity that should be reported publicly. Frank admitted that people would disagree over this standard.

5. Private activity that reveals a pattern of behavior is fair game for reporters. Under this rule, Frank defended the coverage of Gary Hart's sex life during the 1988 presidential race.

6. Different rules apply to Presidential candidates, although no one seems to know what those rules are.

7. Privacy is a shield, not a sword, Frank said. The press ought not protect politicians using their positions to enhance their private activities who then yell, "Privacy." Frank referred to a politician who secures a job for a secret lover. By the same token, having a sexual relationship with someone does not immunize improper activity. The press should not keep quiet, for instance, if it discovers that a sexual partner of a famous person has undue influence on the public figure or has been involved in improper conduct.

8. Certain private information, like a politician's religious views, ought not be reported. The same is true of private information about the families of public officials, according to Frank.

Shortly after articulating these rules, Congressman Frank was confronted with embarrassing disclosures about his private life. He proved that he was willing to abide by his own rules on press coverage and, in the end, he survived the ordeal. Those who do survive these revelations, like Frank, former Representative Geraldine Ferraro, and President Bill Clinton, seem to have a reservoir of good will and political strength to draw on. Those who do not, like Senator Joseph Biden, former Senator Gary Hart, former Senator John Tower, and former House Speaker Jim Wright, apparently can't rely on that.

In other words, voters may excuse almost anything if a politician offers solid achievement and attractive qualities aside from his or her indiscretions.

Frank concluded his presentation on privacy and the press with a rule for politicians: "Tell the truth and nothing but the truth. Tell the whole truth? Well, ... no."

Chapter Eleven
Short Takes

The author, in the course of his advocacy of stronger privacy recognition, delivers regular commentaries on "Marketplace," the early evening consumer/business program on American Public Radio. Here are some of those commentaries, two-minute quick takes on privacy issues of the day.

Lax Fax

What's your assumption when you send a fax?

That the person who is receiving the message is hovering over the machine to seize it and read it.

Of course, that's an erroneous assumption, but one that everybody makes. We assume that the documents we send by facsimile will be seen only by the intended recipient.

And think what we are sending by fax: confidential company memos, medical records, credit reports, sensitive political documents, investigatory materials.

Yet I don't know a single company or government agency that has guidelines on what may and may not be faxed.[1] Nor do I know of an organization that has taken precautions to protect the confidentiality of fax messages they send and those they receive.

It's the great gap in confidentiality right now. We are careful with first class mail and with computer communications and internal memoranda. We have shredding machines and penalties for employees who steal trade secrets. But we don't think twice about transmitting confidential messages by fax — where anyone can pick them up, and read them, and copy them, and send them to someone else by fax.

Not to mention that fax transmissions can be intercepted by wiretaps — just like a phone conversation. In fact, it's easier than tapping a conversation.

The large credit reporting company in Atlanta — Equifax — was embarrassed when a fax message went astray. It described its campaign contribution to the President of the State Senate in California, which was considering legislation beneficial to the company. The home office intended to send it to a lobbyist in Sacramento. By dialing a wrong number, Equifax sent the

---

[1] One exception now is the *Journal of the American Medical Records Association* (now the American Health Information Management Association), which in June 1991 published guidelines for faxing medical information.

embarrassing memo to — oops — the press room in the California capitol.

A company in Minnesota "mis-faxed" a document it called "strictly confidential" concerning a major corporate acquisition. Oops. It sent the fax to *The Wall Street Journal.* The newspaper used the information for a news scoop (using the headline "WE DON'T NORMALLY GET OUR SCOOPS THIS WAY").

K-Mart Corp. misdirected a confidential memo to a supplier, who then noticed a major discrepancy about commissions and filed a successful lawsuit against K-Mart for $73 million.

You would think these horror stories would lead American companies to take extreme precautions in sending out facsimiles. But they haven't.

There are security precautions available. Fax messages can be coded, and recipients' machines can be fitted with personalized keys. Messages can at least be logged and accounted for. And highly confidential material can always be sent by overnight express.

But lax fax continues.

Cat And Mouse

The story of American business is the cat-and-mouse chase by advertisers seeking out consumers. Just when we think we have found a safe haven, the advertisers follow, in hot pursuit.

One of the pleasures of watching baseball in Fenway Park in Boston, for me, was the green, natural respite from commercials. That's no longer true, of course; you can't even check the score in any modern sports stadium without being exposed to advertising.

Public television and public radio used to be safe havens, but commercialism creeps in there as well. The Olympics used to be free of advertising, but no more. T-shirts and *The National Geographic* used to be commercial free.

An entrepreneur has even sold space advertising on the back doors of rest rooms in airplanes. Talk about a captive audience!

It's always interested me that advertisers haven't reached another 10-second captive audience — those of us riding in elevators. I would be receptive to reading advertising there; I have nothing else to do. God knows, no one ever talks in elevators.

Consumers begrudgingly accept these new incursions into their peace and quiet. But I wonder how much more tolerant consumers will be, before they yell, "We're mad as hell. We're not going to take it any more." Remote control devices and video recorders now give us the ability to tune out commercials on television.

I think I have found the outer limits. One is advertising on food — not about food, not on the packaging, but *on* food.

Technologists in Boston have developed a plastic mold that can stamp discernible holographs on a chocolate bar, for instance. Or on each corn flake. We have accepted labels on bananas and oranges for years, but a picture of Ed McMahon on a piece of prime rib?

Last December, Bell Atlantic, which operates the phone companies from New Jersey to Virginia, purchased a patent for a methodology that will patch advertisements into the four-second pauses between rings in a telephone call. Before long, you could be hearing a jingle for Maxwell House Coffee or Caribbean Cruise Lines while waiting for your friend to answer the telephone.

A test of this advertising in Missouri in 1985 was pretty much a disaster, they say. But the inventor thinks that callers will accept the advertising if they get a discount on their phone service. In fact, Neil Sleevi, the inventor, envisions *free* telephone lines paid for by advertising. Perhaps this will start with pay phones.

Of course, the more we saturate each other with commercial messages, the more diluted each message becomes. Or the more pliant we all become as consumers and citizens.

A Tax On Knowledge

In 1712, the British Parliament imposed a tax on all newspapers and advertisements. Historians agree that this was intended not to raise revenue but to stifle published criticism of the Crown. In 1992, the owners of American newspapers are slowly but surely allowing history to repeat itself.

The Massachusetts legislature, following the British example, imposed a stamp tax on all newspapers and magazines in 1785. There was so much opposition that it was repealed a year later, and — to make sure — Congress proposed the First Amendment four years later.

The point is that the First Amendment was clearly inspired by government infringement on a free press *through taxation, not necessarily through censorship of what was published.*

In the past two decades, the major newspapers and their trade associations have passively allowed states to whittle away at this protection from taxation. The newspapers are quick to be heard when there is a censorship threat by the government. But they are strangely silent when there is a taxation threat.

In Virginia, there's a tax on each morning's *Washington Post.* Since 1991, *The Los Angeles Times* has been taxed at newsstands throughout the state of California. *The New York Times* is taxed in every state that has chosen to place a sales tax on publications.

Mail-order subscriptions may soon be subject to state tax if Congress lifts the ban on interstate taxation.

Where is the press? The editorial alarmists? The richly funded trade associations? The noble First Amendment defenders?

They are pathetically silent. The American Newspaper Publishers Association told me, "Because of limited resources, we don't get involved in each state." Can you imagine James Madison saying, "Because of limited resources, I don't get involved"? Would Lincoln Steffens, the great press muckraker, have said, "I don't want to get involved"?

Clearly the states will say these new taxes are revenue raisers, they are not "taxes on knowledge." They will say these taxes are not tantamount to the "license to publish" that our Founding Fathers fought strongly against.

But taxes on periodicals have, state by state, year by year, become every bit as threatening to free expression as the taxes on newspapers in colonial days. As the U.S. Supreme Court said in 1936, taxes like this "have the effect of curtailing the circulation of newspapers, and particularly the cheaper ones whose readers were generally found among the masses of the people."[2]

Taxes on periodicals really *are* equal to a state-issued license to publish or to broadcast. That violates the First Amendment. The great news organizations should wake up. Let's hear from them.

---

[2] *Grosjean v. American Press Co., Inc.,* 295 U.S. 233 (1936).

Over-Testing For Drugs Makes No Sense

Has anybody noticed that since the big uproar over drug testing in the 1980s, the major corporations have discovered that drug testing hasn't been cost-effective?

It is amazing to discover that among 15,000 urinalysis tests given to federal employees, only *one half of one percent* showed a positive result for drug use. Leave out the federal agency with the highest percentage of positive tests — the overseas Panama Canal Commission with nine percent — and the results are more startling: The number of positive drug tests in the other federal agencies is not even statistically significant. Ranking second in the 1990 figures are civilians at the Department of the Navy, with a mere three percent.

There has been a similar experience in the NCAA's drug testing program for college athletes. In 1991, there was not a single positive test result among 1600 athletes, except in football. Among the football players, only 20 tested positive for drugs — six of them for marijuana and two for prescription drugs. That's less than one percent.

What this shows is that we are devoting lots of resources in the so-called war on drugs to places where there is no significant problem — the federal workplace and college athletics. In the process, we are insulting and harming lots of innocent people, and, of course, ignoring the people at the core of the drug problem.

A study published in the *Journal of the American Medical Association* in 1992 showed that drug testing programs are not cost-effective in organizations where fewer than two or three percent of the people use drugs. Drug testing makes sense only in places where drug use is "rampant," the research shows — usually more than 12 percent of the work force.

But we knew that when the Reagan Administration first forced its mania for drug testing upon us.

Why did corporate America go for it?

The Bush Administration's own Department of Labor said that one third of the companies that began drug testing in 1988 later abandoned it.

It is those companies in the transportation and military-contracting businesses that are doing most of the drug testing these days. And that is because federal policies require them to do it.

Smart companies have discovered that, for them, strong hiring practices, employee assistance programs, and good supervision make sense — not mindless drug testing.

Resources for combatting drug abuse are scarce. We should target them where the problems are, not scatter them where there are no problems.

Pre-Puberty Wizardry

Computer "hackers," usually working out of the privacy of their own bedrooms, are snooping electronically into the data banks of major businesses almost without limit these days.

The youngsters who do their wizardry at their keyboards have barely reached puberty.

The favorite target has been nationwide credit-bureau networks, which store information about individual credit-card accounts. One 13-year-old in Michigan gained access to his father's credit file — which is stored in southern California.

With the credit-card numbers they get by infiltrating the credit bureaus, the kids can charge products and services over the telephone. That is what they have been doing with alarming regularity.

TRW Credit Data, based in Orange County, California, has been victimized several times by hackers who get the TRW access code through underground electronic bulletin boards. In the spring of 1992, TRW's major competitor, Equifax Inc., of Atlanta, was stung by a nationwide ring of teenaged hackers who stole information from Equifax's credit files. The ring, based in San Diego and in Dayton, Ohio, stole names and credit card numbers from Equifax's data base. With the information, the teens made fraudulent purchases on other people's accounts. The youths also broke Personal Identity Number (PIN) codes at automatic teller machines and may have had access to other credit bureaus.

To add insult to injury, the unpaid credit-card accounts of the victims create adverse information in the innocent person's credit reports, which then take months of aggravation and expense to get corrected.

Is computer hacking a menace or is it merely good, clean, harmless fun?

A group created by computer enthusiasts, the Electronic Frontier Foundation based in Cambridge, Massachusetts, says that police and the FBI are overreacting to young computer hackers. They say that law enforcement agencies have ignored long-standing principles about reasonable searches and seizures and about due process — by seizing computer equipment and software. EFF thinks also that free speech is threatened when law enforcement monitors or investigates communications on computer enthusiasts' electronic bulletin boards and message networks.

EFF, established by the founder of Lotus Development Corp., a major software innovator, funded the legal defense of a young Chicago man facing a criminal trial for "stealing" telephone company information that was publicly available to anyone. The charges were dismissed.

Each of us will have to keep a close eye on law enforcement as it pursues these high-tech cases. Stealing information, or even snooping into it, *is* a crime, even if you do it from your bedroom and even if you have not reached adulthood. But heavy-handed police actions against horsing around on personal computer networks without compromising someone else's system could stifle some highly creative minds — minds like the one that founded Lotus.

Across The Atlantic

Civil libertarians and consumer groups have been lobbying for decades for stronger privacy protections. They have had some degree of success. But the strongest impetus for new far-reaching privacy protections in the United States is coming from an unlikely source: the capitals of Europe.

In preparation for the commercial merger of European countries, the European Community has drafted tough guidelines for the member nations to protect personal information stored in data banks — whether governmental or business.

The European Community directive adopts the toughest provisions of data-protection laws now on the books in most European countries — requiring an individual's consent before personal information may be gathered, used and disclosed. One provision that has gotten the attention of American businesses requires anyone to get the permission of national authorities in Europe before exporting personal information to the U.S. or any other country. And permission may be denied if the data-protection authority in the European nation decides that the receiving country does not have privacy-protections that meet European standards. The European directive adds bureaucratic levels for approving the transfer of personal information, and these obstacles may slow down some multi-national exchanges to a halt.

The U.S. has good privacy laws — protecting credit files, federal agency data, school records, telephone solicitation, criminal records, and — in some states — other kinds of personal records. But the U.S. and Canada don't have the overall, omnibus-type protection for *all* kinds of records, which the Europeans prefer. For instance, there are no federal protections for medical or insurance records, employment records, or local government files. Nor do we, like the Europeans and the Canadians, have a privacy-protection office at the highest level of government to run interference for the citizen.

An American company without special permission will now be hard-pressed to process its world-wide payroll in the U.S. or to maintain a customer list of Europeans in the U.S.

This has concerned some American companies, like American Express and Reader's Digest, that regularly do business in Europe. U.S. Representative Bob Wise of West Virginia has proposed legislation to create a Data Protection Board in the federal government here, one way to comply with the new European directive. For a change, corporate lobbyists in Washington are lining up support for this pro-privacy measure, as a way of continuing to do business in Europe.

The danger is that we'll end up with legislation so watered down by business interests that it will represent no more than paperwork compliance with the European initiative. The nudge from Europe represents a real opportunity to draft meaningful, across-the-board protections for the privacy of American citizens.

Your Credit File Doesn't Lie Dormant

What's in your personal credit files?

In most cases, your credit report has your current and past addresses, your phone number, where you work, the charge accounts you have or have had, and how promptly you pay them off. Credit reports also include the monthly balances on your credit-card accounts and on your bank loans and sometimes lawsuits involving you.

Most people expect this information to stay within the credit bureau, except when you apply for credit in the future. How many people with unlisted phone numbers, for instance, want their credit bureau to provide their telephone numbers to others?

But the three major credit bureaus — TRW, Trans Union, and Equifax (CBI) — have discovered that they can enhance their profits by recycling credit information. They take bits and pieces of your credit files and do three things.

They build computer profiles that pretend to help merchants predict who will be a bad credit risk and who will file for bankruptcy in the future. And Trans Union and TRW use information from credit histories to build sophisticated, targeted mail and telephone lists for direct sales. These lists tell mailers not only your telephone number, Social Security number and where you live but also what credit cards you use and what your credit limits are. The lists are also segmented by income brackets, family size, ethnic group, automobile ownership, house size, and other demographic factors.

And, additionally, credit bureaus "pre-screen" lists for credit-card companies and others who sell products by mail or phone. In other words, they run a mailer's list against their credit files and eliminate the bad risks from the solicitation before the mailing.

People are objecting to these additional uses of credit information, and some members of Congress have proposed legislation to limit this. The Federal Trade Commission, which is supposed to regulate the credit bureaus, is hardly aware of these new trends in the industry.

Because of this public concern, one of the Big Three, Equifax (CBI), decided in 1991 to cease extracting information from your credit file for targeted-marketing purposes. This is good news. Will the other two — TRW and Trans Union — get the message? Will Congress enact meaningful reforms of the Fair Credit Reporting Act? Will the Federal Trade Commission get a wake-up call?

What Is Pre-Emption And How Does It Affect Our Credit Reports?

We used to hear a lot about "state's rights" until the 1960s when the term became synonymous with preserving a racist status quo.

But — in our democratic federalism — there's merit in the idea that the national government ought not interfere into the policies of individual states where there is no great need for a uniform, nationwide policy.

The debate is alive in the 1990s under a new name — pre-emption. Pre-emption means that Congress, when it passes a law, will simply invalidate stronger state laws that cover the same subject matter.

Congress came close in 1992 to pre-empting state laws in two important areas, both of them affecting our rights to privacy.

The credit-bureau industry pushed pre-emption in amendments to the federal Fair Credit Reporting Act, which regulates credit bureaus.

California, Maine, Maryland, Massachusetts, New York, Vermont — all have credit-reporting laws that protect consumers more than federal law.

The industry won a vote in the House on pre-emption by two votes. After that, the sponsors of the pro-consumer bill withdrew it rather than risk letting it pass with pre-emption in it.

Members of Congress wanted also to pre-empt state laws restricting Caller ID. That's the new telephone service that displays the number of an incoming call.

Think of yourself as a telephone caller — instead of the recipient of calls — and you can see why you might have an honest and legitimate need to place calls anonymously — to a self-help service or for advice on an embarrassing medical condition or for information about a commercial product. In response to these needs, a dozen states require telephone companies when they offer Caller ID also to offer the free capability to block display of your number. New York and California, for instance.

A bill that passed the Senate Judiciary Committee in 1992 would have pre-empted these sensible state requirements. The Federal Communications Commission considered an order doing the same thing.

States can be laboratories for legislation. They offer the opportunity to test new restrictions and new protections before they are adopted everywhere. In many ways, state legislatures are more responsive to consumer needs than the distant legislature in Washington.

Right now, the states are certainly more sophisticated than Congress on credit reporting and new telephone services.

Pre-emption would be an outrage in these two consumer areas.

"Let's Do It Until We Get Caught"

'   "LET'S DO IT UNTIL WE GET CAUGHT." Sounds like kids playing in the backyard.

In fact, it's the philosophy of the three major credit bureaus in the U.S. — Equifax, Trans Union, and TRW.

Equifax, the oldest company in this business, admitted in 1992 that it often flouts the laws regulating its business.

Although formally admitting no wrongdoing, Equifax said that in interviewing job applicants for other companies it has asked about physical and mental disabilities, prior arrests, drug and alcohol use, and club memberships — questions that usually violate state or federal laws.

Trying to cut corners with the law is a dangerous practice for any business — whether in defense contracting, bribing foreign governments, polluting the water and air, or selling substandard products. It works only when the public is unaware of what is going on and when the government regulatory agency in charge is asleep.

But that's the current situation in the credit-reporting business, which prepares credit reports on consumers.

"Let's do it until we get caught." Here are some other examples:

Trans Union and TRW use personal information from credit files to compile marketing lists, even though the Federal Trade Commission called the practice illegal.[3]

For many years, TRW included a credit ranking in its credit reports but denied that it did so and did not disclose this information to consumers who ask to see their files. The company also listed certain inquiries into a person's credit file in a way that the consumer could not recognize the name of the inquiring company. This violates the Fair Credit Reporting Act. Attorneys General of 18 states finally extracted an agreement from TRW — and later from Equifax and from Trans Union to discontinue the practice.

Although the law requires a credit bureau not to release personal information to a user it believes will misuse it, the Big Three continue to do business with disreputable "information brokers" that they know resell the data to strangers (whose purpose for the information is unknown).

Other examples:

Federal law requires credit bureaus to assure "maximum possible accuracy" of the information they sell, but TRW, Trans Union, and Equifax continue to use the services of a company called National Data Retrieval, which at least twice now has reported erroneous negative information about thousands of homeowners in New England.

Although federal law requires a credit bureau to verify the identity of any user of its credit reports, young computer hackers have easily infiltrated the systems of both Equifax and TRW to steal credit re-

---

[3] In January 1993, the Federal Trade Commission formally cited TRW and Trans Union for violating the law in this respect.

ports. Even independent Presidential candidate Ross Perot's operatives were able to get Equifax credit reports on their 1992 campaign volunteers, in apparent violation of the law.

Now that a more alert public and press have caught the credit bureaus in the act, perhaps the Big Three will straighten up.

Chapter Twelve
Our Privacy Protections Today

Just what is protected by "the right to privacy"?

It's not easy to find out, because privacy is protected by a patchwork quilt of court cases, laws, and constitutional principles.

Privacy is recognized implicitly as a constitutional right. Although the U.S. Supreme Court has severely restricted this constitutional right to privacy in the past two decades, it still recognizes the right especially in matters relating to procreation, child rearing and education, contraception, and family matters.[1]

---

[1] *Griswold v. Connecticut,* 381 U.S. 479 (1965). *Roe v. Wade,* 410 U.S. 113 (1973). *Paul v. Davis,* 424 U.S. 693 (1976).

In other words, there remains a constitutional right to free choice and confidentiality, as against governmental intrusion, in those areas of our personal lives. Governmental practices that restrict these activities could violate the constitutional right to privacy.

Think what sensitive areas of our lives are *not* covered: homosexual or pre-marital sexual activity, financial information, medical information, our selection of hair styles and clothes (or lack of them), or the shielding of our bodily functions, like urination.

In its 1992 opinion reaffirming the right to an abortion, the Supreme Court again found protected zones of privacy, but called them *liberty*. Within this protected zone is the "private realm of family life," as well as "the right to define one's own concept of existence, of the meaning of the universe, and of the mystery of human life." Associate Justice Sandra Day O'Connor, writing for the majority of the court, used the word "personhood" to define this realm of privacy.[2]

Privacy is recognized *explicitly* in the constitutions of a few states — including Alaska, Arizona, California, Florida, Hawaii, Louisiana, Montana, South Carolina, and Washington.[3] In California and Montana, state supreme courts have said that the state constitutional right to privacy goes beyond the reach of the federal right, and it even applies to private entities as well as the government.

In California the state Supreme Court said, "The right of privacy is the right to be left alone. It is a fundamental and compelling interest. It protects our

---

[2] *Planned Parenthood v. Casey,* 60 *US Law Week* 4795 (1992).
[3] For listings of all laws and constitutional protections on privacy, see *Compilation of State and Federal Privacy Laws,* published by *Privacy Journal,* PO Box 28577, Providence, RI 02908.

homes, our families, our thoughts, our emotions, our expressions, our personalities, our freedom of communion and our freedom to associate with whom we choose. It prevents government *and business interests* from collecting and stockpiling unnecessary information about us and from misusing information gathered for one purpose in order to serve other purposes or embarrass us... The proliferation of government *and business records* over which we have no control limits our ability to control our personal lives." [Emphasis added.]⁴

In addition to the contitutional protections, the right to privacy is recognized in the following federal statutes:

The Federal Privacy Act of 1974, which limits the disclosure of personal information held by federal agencies and permits individuals to have copies of most federal information concerning them.

The Federal Fair Credit Reporting Act, which provides the same rights with regard to credit bureaus and other companies that provide consumer-type personal information to employers, insurance companies, and others.

The Family Educational Rights and Privacy Act of 1974, which provides the same rights with regard to student records held by schools and universities receiving federal money.

The Right to Financial Privacy Act of 1978, which requires federal investigators to present proper legal process to inspect the financial records of an individual in a bank or other financial institution. In most cases, the customer is entitled to advance notice when his or her records are inspected.

---

⁴ *White v. Davis,* 533 P 2d 222 (1975).

The Video Privacy Protection Act, which limits disclosure of the identity of videotapes rented to individuals.

The Cable Television Privacy Law, which protects personal information stored by local cable providers.

The Electronic Communications Privacy Act of 1986 and the federal wiretap law of 1968, which prohibit electronic surveillance unless there is a warrant or the consent of one party to a telephone conversation.

The Employee Polygraph Protection Act of 1988, which bans most polygraph tests by private employers, especially in the application stage.

The Telephone Consumer Protection Act of 1991, which prohibits telemarketers from calling an individual who has notified them that he or she does not wish to receive such calls, as well as putting other restrictions on telemarketers.

State laws protect other areas. Many states protect the confidentiality of arrest information if there is no guilty finding or the first offense is a minor one. A handful of states say that bank records are confidential. Some have laws on credit reports stricter than the federal Fair Credit Reporting Act.

A total of 15 states now provide protection for personal information held by state agencies and permit a person to inspect his or her own files and to correct them.

Insurance records are partially protected in 12 states, with laws that are not very strong. Only a very few states have laws regarding medical information as confidential, although most states have language in their laws specifying confidentiality of information about AIDS patients and persons who have been tested for the virus. About 20 states have laws permitting patients access to their own medical files.

Some states — but fewer than a dozen — provide employees a right to see their own personnel files.

All states but Vermont punish unauthorized access into a computer system or the use of a computer in a crime.

Most states have laws on student records, although this area is pretty well covered by the federal law. In recent years, legislatures in 30 states have regulated the time and manner for companies to use automated dialing devices or recordings to solicit sales (another area now dominated by federal law). And two-thirds of the states have restrictions on electronic eavesdropping similar to federal law.

As most people know, our legal system has long recognized the confidentiality of information shared with a lawyer or clergy, physician, or psychotherapist. But these are limited protections; they do not extend to all communications.

The right to privacy is also recognized in "tort law," when one private party intrudes upon the solitude of another or discloses private facts about that person. Since the early part of this century, states have passed laws recognizing a right to sue for invasions of privacy if someone misappropriates your name or face for commercial profit or discloses sensitive information without any rational purpose. Sometimes courts, not legislatures, have created such a right to sue.

What's missing?

States provide shockingly limited protection for a person's medical information — and ironically give no rights for a patient to even know exactly what is in medical files about himself or herself. And employees are vulnerable — no rights to confidentiality, no rights of access to their personnel files (in most places), and no protections against most snooping by private companies. This is especially important in the last decade of the Twentieth Century because new advances in genetic research permit employers or insurance companies to discover traits in a person's make-up that show a predilection to certain diseases or irregular genetic conditions. In this emerging area, there are no legal protections for the rights of the individual.

Chapter Thirteen
Twenty Principles To Protect Information Privacy

The information mongers among us are constantly saying, "Privacy is a vague concept. It means different things to different people."

That may be true to the information mongers. Their usual reaction, after all, is to say that their systems are secure and responsibly managed. They believe that they have considered privacy protections and that people have no need to worry.

In fact, privacy is not a vague concept. Over the past two decades a substantial amount of study has gone into information-privacy issues — always with an eye to developing principles that will guide those who develop information systems. Some of the principles that follow in this chapter have widespread support among experts in the privacy field; others are fairly new and untested. For the guidance of both information collectors and the people who are the subjects of that information collection, here are principles for the protection of personal privacy, annotated afterwards with their sources:

1.   There must be no personal-information systems whose very existence is secret.

2.   There must be a way for a person to find out what information about him or her is in a record and how it is used.

3.   There must be a way for a person to prevent personal information that was obtained for one purpose from being used or made available for other purposes without the consent of the person.

4.   There must be a way for a person to correct or amend a record of identifiable information about himself or herself.

5.   Any organization creating, maintaining, using, or disseminating records of identifiable personal data must assure the reliability of the information for its intended use and must take precautions to prevent misuse of the data.

6.   Any system of records about people must have a purpose that is socially desirable, and only relevant information should be collected.

7.   To the maximum extent, personal information should be gathered from the individual himself or herself.

8.   The keepers of personal information should act in the role of trustee, safeguarding the information and using it in the best interests of the individual, but not *owning* it.

9. Privacy   interests   should   be   considered specifically in the design and creation of new data

systems, communications services, and other new technology that affects the interests of individuals.

10. Privacy protections, as much as possible, should be tailored to the needs of each individual, and each individual should be able to choose from among various degrees of privacy protection, perhaps bearing an additional cost for special services.

11. A company or government agency that compromises current expectations of privacy should be obligated to offer a means of restoring the lost degree of privacy at no cost to consumers.

12. Information provided to a business or government agency by a person should be used only in connection with services or benefits sought by the person, unless the person agrees otherwise.

13. Privacy expectations may change over time, as new technology, new markets, new attitudes, and new social concerns emerge.

14. When information is disclosed for commercial purposes, an individual ought to have a means to "opt out" by having his or her information not disclosed.

15. The concept of privacy applies only to actual persons, not to organizations. It applies only to information that identifies an individual (by name, number or otherwise) not to cumulative or anonymous information.

16. Privacy problems lend themselves to negotiation and complaint resolution, often on a case-by-case basis, rather than hard-and-fast legal language.

17. Personal information provided to a third party (for processing or billing or research) is governed by the same protections applicable to the original keeper of the records.

18. Personal information may be transferred from one jurisdiction to another only if the second jurisdic-

tion has privacy protections at least equal to those of the first, unless the first jurisdiction provides special permission.

19. Information used by a government agency should be available to citizens in two formats: in the media (whether electronic or otherwise) used by the agency itself and in a form that is usable and readable to a person without electronic media.

20. In the absence of factual suspicion, overhearing private conversations or viewing people's personal activities from afar with technological enhancements is unethical.

The first five principles were originated by a study committee in the U.S. Department of Health, Education, and Welfare in 1973, and endorsed later by an IBM Corp. study and by the organization of Computer Professionals for Social Responsibility. This "Code of Fair Information Practices" appears again and again in laws passed since 1973, including the Privacy Act, state fair information practices acts, and national laws enacted by European countries.

Principle Six has been promoted in Europe. It is part of the 1981 privacy guidelines of the Organization for Economic Cooperation and Development (OECD) in Europe. The concept of relevance has been difficult to articulate in legislation.

Principle Seven is part of the Privacy Act.

There is less agreement about Principle Eight, which is often suggested, but is not yet a part of any recognized code of practice.

Versions of Principles Nine through Thirteen were published in 1991 by the New York State Public Service Commission, under the leadership of Commissioner Eli Noam. Principles Ten and Eleven together mean that customers or citizens should not have to pay to preserve the privacy status quo but that customers or citizens who choose a greater degree of protection should expect to bear at least part of the cost themselves. Many European nations have adopted a variation of Principle Twelve, saying that an individual is entitled to know from the beginning the purpose for information he or she is asked to provide.

Principle Fourteen is promoted by the direct-marketing industry and others to head off more restrictive requirements. It begs the questions of whether people know the consequences of opting out or not opting out and whether the information should be collected or disclosed at all. Some say that it places the burden on the individual; they prefer an "opt-in" provision, whereby information could not be disclosed unless an individual affirmatively consented; others say that "opt-out" preserves the free flow of personal information in commerce.

The first part of Principle Fifteen is a general concept of American law. Businesses may have *an interest in secrecy or confidentiality,* but this is different from the uniquely individual *right* of privacy. In Europe, however, some federal laws cover corporations (known as "legal persons," to distinguish them from "natural persons"). The second part of the principle is found in the definitions section of the federal Privacy Act. It makes clear that privacy legislation applies only when personal information may be retrieved by a name or other identifier.

In the U.S., there is no general agreement on Principle Sixteen, which seems to guide policy makers in Europe, Australia, and Canada.

Principle Seventeen, part of the federal Privacy Act, assures that processing or research organizations merely act as the agent of the original organization when it comes to handling personal information entrusted to the third party. As a condition of using information from the first organization, the third party agrees to be bound by the first organization's privacy safeguards. Any disclosure or additional use of the information by the third party violates this principle.

Principle Eighteen is required by law in Austria, Denmark, France, Sweden, and the United Kingdom and is part of guidelines drafted by the European Community to apply to all European countries.

Principle Nineteen is a concept of freedom of information developed by the author.

Principle Twenty represents essentially the current law in the U.S. with regard to electronic eavesdropping. On the matter of video surveillance and covert videotaping, courts are currently groping for proper principles.

Afterword:
Working Alone

People are always telling me, "You must have a lot of self-discipline." That's because for the past two decades, I have worked at home, often alone. My deadlines are self-imposed; the demands on my time are my own, not someone else's.

I began publishing a monthly newsletter about the right to privacy on my own in 1974, in an office above the garage behind my home seven blocks from the U.S. Capitol in Washington. In 1985, when I moved back to Rhode Island, I discovered that my business was perfectly portable. We packed it in boxes and transferred it without missing a beat.

Now I work out of a secluded office on the third floor of my home in Providence, RI.

No one interrupts me with office gossip or petty politics. I don't have to connive for a parking place. It's been a long time since I was compelled to attend an office party. And it's been almost two decades since I was pressured into contributing to a charitable campaign I cared nothing about.

This allows more time for the substance of my work. The commuting distance is about right — after a second cup of coffee and a leisurely look through the morning papers, I simply climb a flight of stairs and arrive way ahead of people fighting the morning traffic.

And the rewards are many. When I succeed I know that I — on my own — succeeded; when I fail I don't get resentful blaming someone else — or something else.

I strongly identify with the comments of Orson Welles, the independent film producer and actor, to a Hollywood audience: "There are a few of us left in this conglomerated world of ours who still trudge stubbornly along the lonely, rocky road and this is our 'contrarity.'

"We don't move nearly as fast as our cousins on the freeway. We don't get as much accomplished, just as the family-sized farm can't possibly raise as many crops or get as much profit as the agricultural factory of today. What we do come up with has no special right to call itself better. It's just different. No, if there's any excuse for us at all it's just that we're simply following the old American tradition of the maverick. And we are a vanishing breed. A maverick may go his own way but he doesn't think it's the only way or ever claim that it's the best one — except maybe for himself. And don't imagine that this raggle-taggle gypsy is claiming to be free. It's just that some of the necessities to which I am a slave are different from yours."

I agree with most of Orson Welles' homily but not all of it. "We don't get as much accomplished"? I think that independent self-employed persons often accomplish more than their corporate counterparts. We have fewer distractions, fewer obligations to get approvals or go-aheads from others in the organization. We just *do it*. In my chosen field, I've never had difficulty competing with large companies or government agencies. Consider this book, for instance. I'm sure that I've been able to produce it a lot sooner than if I had done it within a corporate structure.

And I don't agree necessarily with Orson Welles that "we are a dying breed." Computer and telecommunications technologies now allow more people to produce as independent entrepreneurs or consultants, often getting the bulk of their business from the very companies they once worked for.

It's interesting to me that the other individuals producing significant work in the privacy/information technology area are also self-employed, usually working at home — Alan F. Westin, Evan Hendricks, Stewart Dresner, Thomas B. Riley, Harry Hamitt. The other leading persons in this field are doing practically the same thing — Marc Rotenberg, David H. Flaherty, Gary T. Marx.

This is no coincidence, I'm sure. It is easier, surely, to champion a right to privacy this way than amid the clutter of a high-rise corporate work area. Privacy buffs don't generally join large groups.

The great reward of my particular work style has been that I spend my time researching, writing, and debating about a basic American value — the right to privacy. It's a right closely akin to the solitude, the reflection, and the friendship of self that characterize this work style.

By writing books, articles, and a monthly newsletter about privacy, I have been thrilled to deal with crucial constitutional values every day at work. It's been like having Thomas Jefferson, James Madison, and Louis Brandeis looking over my shoulder when I sit down at the word processor. They have turned out to be fine co-workers.

Index

YOU WILL ALSO WANT TO READ: